A CASEBOOK FOR SCHOOL LEADERS

Linking the ISLLC Standards to Effective Practice

Third Edition

Karen L. Hanson
National University

PEARSON

Merrill
Prentice Hall

Upper Saddle River, New Jersey
Columbus, Ohio

Library of Congress Cataloging-in-Publication Data

Hanson, Karen L.
  A casebook for school leaders : linking the ISLLC standards to effective practice
Karen L. Hanson.—3rd ed.
    p. cm.
  Rev. ed. of: Preparing for educational administration using case analysis. 2005.
  Includes bibliographical references and index.
  ISBN 978-0-13-612682-9
 1. School administrators—Training of—United States. 2. School management and
organization—United States—Case studies. 3. School administrators—United States—Case
studies. I. Hanson, Karen L. Preparing for educational administration using case analysis.
II. Interstate School Leaders Licensure Consortium. III. Title.
  LB1738.5.H35 2009
  371.200973—dc22

               2007046101

Vice President and Executive Publisher: Jeffery W. Johnston
Executive Editor: Darcy Betts Prybella
Editorial Assistant: Nancy J. Holstein
Production Editor: Sarah N. Kenoyer
Production Coordinator: Kelly Ricci/Aptara, Inc.
Design Coordinator: Diane C. Lorenzo
Cover Design: Ali Mohrman
Cover Image: Jupiter Images
Production Manager: Susan W. Hannahs
Director of Marketing: Quinn Perkson
Marketing Coordinator: Brian Mounts

This book was set in 10/14 New Aster by Aptara Inc. It was printed and bound by R. R. Donnelley
& Sons Company. The cover was printed by Phoenix Color Corp.

Pearson Education Ltd.   Pearson Education Australia Pty. Limited
Pearson Education Singapore Pte. Ltd.   Pearson Education North Asia Ltd.
Pearson Education Canada, Ltd.   Pearson Educación de Mexico, S.A. de C.V.
Pearson Education–Japan   Pearson Education Malaysia Pte. Ltd.

10 9 8 7 6 5 4 3 2 1
ISBN-13:   978-0-13-612682-9
ISBN-10:   0-13-612682-0

To my grandchildren, who remind me every day that the human experience can be enriched by the stories we tell, the problems we solve, and the lessons we learn.

PREFACE

This book was written for individuals who are interested in pursuing a career in educational administration. It offers a unique opportunity to engage in case analysis, meaningful discussion, lively debate, and serious problem solving with case material that is relevant and realistic and that captures the interest of the reader. The primary purpose of the book is to introduce cases that represent real-life situations in today's schools and to provide a case analysis framework as a tool for analyzing the cases and resolving the problem(s) presented in each case.

The book is a valuable resource for university professors, educational administration students, school districts, county offices of education, group seminar leaders, and specific workshop trainers who believe, as I do, that theory without practice is a waste of time for individuals who aspire to become educational administrators.

The 44 cases presented in the text provide practical experiences in case analysis for individuals who are preparing for educational administration, and they motivate students to pursue research for additional information to adequately address the problems identified in the cases. The cases represent diverse and culturally rich examples of some of the issues school administrators experience. Included are traditional subjects such as curriculum and instruction, leadership, employee and community relations, budget and finance, governance, politics, and law, student conduct, technology and the web, and special education. Also included are more sensitive subjects such as race and ethnic relations, security, health and welfare, ethics, diversity, and gender issues.

ISLLC Standards

The matrix that appears on the inside front cover is designed to correlate the subject matter in the cases with the Interstate School Leaders Licensure Consortium (ISLLC) model standards for school leaders and to identify specific topics addressed in each case. The matrix provides a valuable resource for individuals who wish to apply case studies literature to educational leadership standards research.

Case Organization

Each case has four specific sections. The first section focuses on the people, place, and culture of the school community and provides background for the case. The second section introduces a problem or problems that need to be resolved, and the third section offers questions that are intended to guide the student through the problem-solving process. The questions also serve to prompt students to consider additional strategies for resolving the various problems that are presented. The fourth and final section lists one or more activities that are designed to help students further develop their problem-solving skills and practice what they have learned as a result of the case analysis process.

The case analysis framework in the Introduction provides a tool for systematically processing the information in the cases, categorizing the data, summarizing the material, and locating the source of the primary case problem so the problem-solving process can begin. The framework helps isolate the problem and helps readers respond effectively to the questions at the end of each case.

An example of how to use and apply the case analysis framework appears after the first case, "Is There a Nurse in the House?"

Although the book is intended to be fiction and all the names are fictitious, many of the cases present very real possibilities, and some of them portray events similar to those experienced by educational leaders in schools across the United States.

As students read the cases and use the case analysis framework, they will develop a unique foundation of skills for addressing the challenges that school leaders experience. This book is a must-read for students of educational leadership who wish to take on this challenge of providing a quality educational environment for children.

New to This Edition

This edition includes the following additions:

- An emphasis on Interstate School Leaders Licensure Consortium (ISLLC) standards
- New sections titled "Developing Your Leadership Expertise"

- Five new cases focusing on the following subject matter:
  - Separation of church and state
  - Personal leadership development
  - No Child Left Behind
  - Fund-raising
  - Leadership attributes
- Revised questions and activities to include higher-level thinking questions and inquiry-based activities

Acknowledgments

I wish to express my deepest appreciation to my husband, Gregory, who stood by me when I was tired and offered endless hours of editing—not to mention a good cup of coffee when I needed it.

I wish to thank the following individuals who contributed substantially to the development, content, and story lines for some of the cases in this book: Gary Hoban, Lynne Anderson, John Carta-Falsa, Mark Miller, Bernard Balanay, Roberta Rose, Julie Burke, Maria Castilleja, Timothy Glover, Deborah Huggins, R. Y. Jackson, Gloria McKearney, Suzanne Miyasaki, Staci Monreal, C. Pebley, Linda Rees, Mel Schuler, Tom Spence, Margaret Steinrichter, Nancy Intermill, Deborah Costanzo, Shelley Peterson, Linda Choy, Karen Mooney, Kyle Ruggles, Julie Burke, F. Steve Kennedy, Jr., Katie Langford, Cheryl Bowen, Laurie Francis, and Rae Correira.

The reviewers of this book provided valuable insight: Sue Abbeglan, Culver-Stockton College; Abe Lujau Armendariz, New Mexico State University; Marna L. Beard, Saginaw Valley State University; Casey Brown, Texas A&M University; and Rhoda B. Tillman, Wilkes University.

Finally, I would like to extend my gratitude to Darcy Betts Prybella, Executive Editor, who offered valuable guidance and support.

Contents

INTRODUCTION

The Context

The primary responsibility of school leaders is to oversee the operation of educational institutions to ensure that teachers teach and students learn. The challenges that administrators face can be overwhelming because of an influential and politically motivated environment that demands more than simply an allegiance to teaching and learning. School administrators need to learn how to balance theory with practice—the ideal with reality—and how to establish a middle ground on which to operate.

A career in school administration is particularly difficult at the current time because of a multitude of influences affecting students and teachers. Classroom teachers, students, and school leaders are intensely scrutinized by individuals from all walks of life who claim to have the remedy for what ails education. Partnerships between public and private schools, collaborations between industry and education, and a controversial union of state and religious interests are some examples of influences that affect the way schools operate.

The situation is further complicated because the infrastructure that supports education in America is fragmented and lacks the structural continuity needed to facilitate the transformation that is taking place. As an example, the decision makers in the United States have not agreed on whether national performance standards for students should be applied at the state level or how state-mandated standards should work with federal standards. Some states use the state-mandated curriculum frameworks and textbooks, whereas other states allow local schools to create their own curricula and expect teachers to choose the textbooks students use.

There is an ongoing controversy surrounding student performance. How should teachers assess students? What tests should be administered? How should test scores be interpreted to measure academic competency? Furthermore, the discussion concerning norm-referenced versus criterion-referenced tests and which tests are preferred to measure performance outcomes is far from being resolved. Additionally, the issue of grade-level exam requirements is unresolved, as is the coordination of local, state, and federal examinations to reflect consistent assessment.

The United States lacks a uniform policy that addresses the collection and distribution of revenue to support its educational system, in spite of the commitment to the No Child Left Behind mandate. Inequity exists between states and also between districts within some states in terms of the money spent per child to educate students in schools.

Program initiatives such as parental choice and the voucher system create an imbalance in the education status quo. Legislators and business interests complicate the ongoing deliberation by competing for political and financial profit—for instance, by promoting the use of public funds for private school placement including religious schools. In addition, representatives from special-interest groups have gained support in recent years by running for school board positions and by supporting elected officials who sympathize with their causes.

Adding to this unstable condition are teacher-training programs that reflect major inconsistencies. For example, in some states, a fifth year in an institution of higher education is mandated by accreditation agencies for teacher certification, whereas other states have no such requirement. Furthermore, a few states require additional tests in subject matter curriculum for certification, whereas other states do not.

Future teachers are discouraged by these discrepancies in the system, and the United States is slow in responding to the challenges that many states face as the demand for new teachers increases because of early teacher retirement, a high rate of teacher turnover, and insufficient salaries to recruit the best and brightest candidates for the teaching profession. Adding to teacher dissatisfaction, methods for evaluating teacher performance vary considerably.

Today's schools need strong leadership and well-prepared and educated administrators who understand the complexity of the educational system, can solve problems, and have the commitment to raise the benchmark for educational programs and performance in U.S. schools.

We need caring professionals who are willing and able to take on the challenges that school leadership brings. Individuals who sign up for the job of educational administrators face an exciting time. They will be challenged to advance creative ideas, to preserve successful policies and programs, and to solve problems that otherwise would prevent them from accomplishing their goals.

The Cases

In order to prepare for their futures, teachers who have the goal of becoming educational administrators will benefit from analyzing cases that represent different types of problems occurring in schools. The matrix illustrated on the inside front cover outlines specific topics of concern to educational administrators and identifies the cases that particularly address those issues. The cases are intended to stimulate classroom discussion, to encourage problem solving, and to promote an interest in the research needed to advance an understanding of the content and problems introduced.

The Purpose

It is worthwhile to remember that the value of analyzing cases is to enhance the practical side of preparing for educational administration while relying on meaningful research to strengthen the problem-solving experience. Combining theory and practice offers a realistic balance to the educational administration process, and it fosters a dedication to understanding the research as it applies to everyday life. School administrators are individuals who welcome these challenges, commit to the charge, and believe that children are worth it.

Analyzing case studies to prepare for a career as an educational administrator can be a useful exercise in the art of problem solving. Attend to the cases. If you simply read the cases and answer the questions, you may not develop the insight and appreciation of knowledge or gain in internalizing the case study to improve your problem-solving skills. The cases should be treated as real situations, and the analysis should be undertaken with the intention of actually making decisions and resolving the problems at issue.

FIGURE 1 Hanson's Case Analysis Framework

HANSON'S CASE ANALYSIS FRAMEWORK

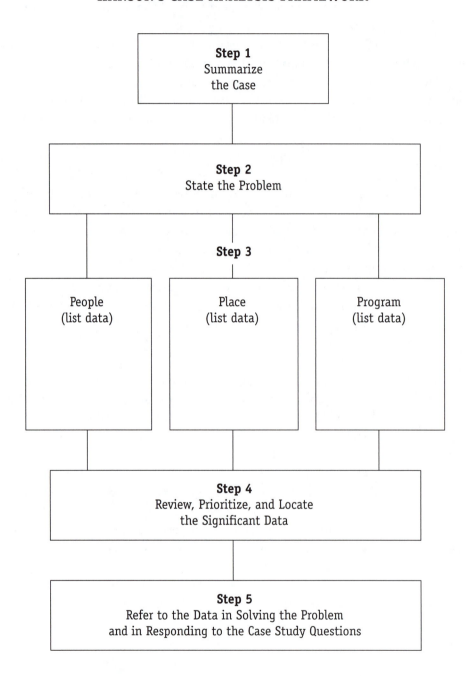

Hanson's Case Analysis Framework

I have designed a case analysis framework (see Figure 1) to assist you in analyzing the cases. The process of analyzing the cases is detailed in the following steps:

1. Summarize the case.
2. Identify the problem in a single sentence.
3. Select specific information from the case and categorize it according to people, place, or program.
4. Review and prioritize the information.
5. Refer to the data in each category to solve the problem identified in the case and to respond to the case study questions.

An example of how to use the case analysis framework is provided at the end of Case 1, "Is There a Nurse in the House?"

Each case offers a different background with a unique problem to solve. Depending on the specifics of the case, it is possible that the most significant data are either concentrated in one of the three categories (people, place, program) or contained in a combination of two or more categories.

As a final note, you are encouraged to conduct appropriate research and investigate district, state, and federal mandates that relate to each case to develop a responsible foundation for analyzing the cases and solving the problems presented.

As future educational leaders, it is up to you to meet the challenge.

IS THERE A NURSE IN THE HOUSE?

The population of Summerset is growing at a rapid pace, and new housing developments are continually being built for moderate- to high-income families. The community has become a close partner with the school district and participates in the district's annual summit meetings, where specific goals and objectives are established. Community members actively support individual schools by promoting funding initiatives and by volunteering to work in the schools.

Challenger School District is located in the heart of Summerset and serves approximately 50,000 students. Although 70% of the school district's population is Hispanic, Discovery High School, which is the only high school in the district, reflects a more ethnically balanced population. The school provides educational services for a population of 35% Hispanic, 30% Caucasian, 20% Pacific Islanders, and 15% African American students.

With an enrollment of 1,900 students, Discovery High provides a variety of programs to students in Grades 9 through 12. Additionally, it provides support for students with special needs, particularly for the gifted and talented students, for those with limited English proficiency, and for students with other special education needs.

The high school staff includes 120 teachers, 3 assistant principals, 5 counselors, 2 part-time campus security staff, an itinerant psychologist, and the usual classified support personnel. The school is highly regarded in the community because of the faculty's commitment to interdisciplinary teaching. Students also have the opportunity to focus their studies in specific areas of interest such as fine arts, multimedia, technology, and engineering.

School activities and events are widely featured in two of the most popularly read newspapers and are highlighted on the local television station. School board members visit the site frequently, and at least three of them are currently running for city council. The school board members are divided on numerous issues, including personnel, school operations, race relations, and program funding.

The superintendent is serving his second year, prior to which he was employed as the assistant superintendent in the same school district.

Special interest groups have had a strong influence on the election of school board members and the selection of superintendents. Included in the list of influential groups are the Latino Coalition, the Special Education Parent Advocate Group, and the 504 Disability Act Committee.

For this case, assume that you are one of the assistant principals at Discovery High School.

The Problem

The school principal and two of your colleagues, who are also assistant principals, are attending a state conference off-site for four days. The principal has charged you with managing the school and has specifically requested that you address a problem with one of the parents, Mrs. Carlton.

Two of her sons, John and Abraham, are enrolled at the high school, and they both have cerebral palsy. They have attended Discovery High for the past two years. Each one of Mrs. Carlton's sons is an excellent student, and they are both enrolled in honors classes and have been mainstreamed into regular education classes for the entire school day. A registered nurse is assigned to each of the boys. During school hours, the nurses are available to tend to the boys' needs and are compensated by the school district.

Mrs. Carlton has issued several verbal complaints to the principal and the special education program director regarding John's nurse, Mrs. Adams. According to Mrs. Carlton, Mrs. Adams is often late when meeting John's bus in the morning, and so the bus leaves for John's school without Mrs. Adams. Mrs. Carlton is concerned because, even though her other son's nurse is on the school bus, there have been times when both boys needed medical attention simultaneously. In the past, some situations have been so severe that Mrs. Carlton has described them as medical emergencies.

A few months ago, Mrs. Carlton issued a written complaint requesting the dismissal of Mrs. Adams. The principal met with John's parents and Mrs. Adams to discuss the situation, and an agreement was reached to assign Mrs. Adams to another school in the district. In the meantime, Mrs. Carlton decided to keep John at home until the school district found a new nurse for him. The district informed Mrs. Carlton that it would take at least eight weeks to hire a new nurse.

In the principal's absence, you decide to address Mrs. Carlton's concerns by locating a teacher in the school who is willing to work at John's home with him. In addition, you suggest to the special education program director that she contact a temporary employment agency in town who you believe has nurses available for immediate placement.

The director of special education contacts your office to inform you that the agency has a nurse available for employment. She also informs you that the school district's director of human resources has agreed to hire the nurse from the agency.

You decide to contact Mrs. Carlton immediately and share the good news with her. She is delighted that John will be able to return to Discovery High School and that a new nurse will be assigned to him.

Before John returns to school, the director of human resources contacts you by phone to inform you that he has thought about the situation and now refuses to accept the nurse from the agency for employment. He reminds you that the school site principal is away at a conference and that it would be inappropriate for a decision of this magnitude to be made in his absence.

When you request that he contact Mrs. Carlton and explain the change in plans, he refuses and makes it clear to you that it is your responsibility as the administrator in charge to make the call. You do so, and, of course, Mrs. Carlton is very upset. She tells you that she plans to attend the next school board meeting and bring both of her sons with her as well as a special education parent advocate and a local television news station reporter.

Sample Case Analysis Application

Step 1
Summarize the Case
Mrs. Carlton is a parent with two sons who have special needs and who attend Discovery High School. She has filed a complaint because she wants the nurse

assigned to one of her sons to be replaced by another nurse. You are the assistant principal charged with handling the complaint while the principal is off campus.

Discovery High School has a balanced ethnic population of students in Grades 9 through 12, and the community is very supportive of the school.

The school board members visit the school often, and special interest groups have a strong influence on the board members. The school board is divided on many issues including personnel.

In response to Mrs. Carlton's complaint against a school nurse, district office personnel have been inconsistent in honoring her request to hire a new nurse for her son.

Mrs. Carlton plans to attend the next school board meeting along with her two sons, a special education parent advocate, and a representative from the media.

Step 2
Identify the Problem in a Single Sentence
The significance of identifying the problem is that it allows you to focus on the most important issue. In this case, the problem can be identified as Mrs. Carlton wanting a new nurse to be hired for her son and that she is going to take her complaint to the school board.

Step 3
Select Significant Information and Place the Data into the Categories
The category *People* includes customs, norms, personalities, race, gender, sources of political power, and so on. The *Place* category includes location, physical condition, demographics, rural versus suburban, and so on. *Program* includes curriculum, grade level, type of program (e.g., special education, bilingual), private versus public.

For this case the following apply:

People
1. Mrs. Carlton is a parent of two sons who have special needs, and she is dissatisfied with the nurse assigned to one of her sons.
2. You are the assistant principal charged with handling Mrs. Carlton's complaint.

3. The school district representative has changed his mind about hiring a new nurse for Mrs. Carlton's son.
4. There is a great deal of community support through funding and volunteer work.
5. School board members visit the site frequently.
6. Various issues, including hiring personnel, employee transfers, managing racial conflicts, and funding programs, divide the school board.
7. Special interest groups have a strong impact on the school board.
8. Influential groups include the Latino Coalition, the Special Education Parent Advocate Group, and the 504 Disability Act Committee.
9. Mrs. Carlton is taking her complaint to the school board.

Place

1. The school district is at the center of the community.
2. There is an increase in new housing developments in the community.
3. The population of the community is growing.
4. The socioeconomic description is moderate to high income.
5. Seventy percent of the community is Hispanic, and the school population is balanced.

Program

1. The school serves students in Grades 9 through 12.
2. Teachers participate in interdisciplinary teaching.
3. The school has many strong, special programs, including those for special education, fine arts, multimedia, technology, and engineering.
4. Programs are often featured in the newspaper and on the local television station.

Step 4
Review and Prioritize the Data: Identify the Category that Contains the Most Significant Information Leading to the Problem

1. You are the assistant principal in charge while the principal is away from the school at a conference.
2. Mrs. Carlton is taking her complaint for a new nurse for her son to the school board.
3. The school board is divided by many issues.

4. Among the groups that influence the school board are the 504 Disability Act Committee and the Special Education Parent Advocate Group.

In this case, the category *People* contains the most significant information about the problem. The location and other factors related to place are not the most significant factors, nor is the program as significant as the people, even though the students in this case are enrolled in special education classes. The problems surrounding the nurse and the conflict over the nurse are the main issues.

Step 5
Refer to the Data in Step 4 to Solve the Problem Presented in the Case and to Respond to the Case Study Questions

Mrs. Carlton, who is planning to attend the next school board meeting with a complaint, has the support of an influential group at a school where the principal is absent and the media is concerned about what happens.

Now that you have completed the process, answer the questions for the case and refer to the final steps to help you resolve the problem. Pay particular attention to the conclusion(s) drawn from the data, which will help you to respond to the questions.

Case Analysis Framework
1. Summarize the case.
2. Identify the problem in a single sentence.
3. Select specific information from the case and categorize it according to people, place, or program.
4. Review and prioritize the information.
5. Refer to the data in each category to solve the problem identified in the case and to respond to the case study questions.

Questions to Research and Consider
1. What is the first thing you would do in this situation?
2. What do you foresee happening at the school board meeting?
3. Who do you think will be blamed for the problem with John's nurse?
4. What could you have done differently?

5. What is the best solution for John's well-being?
6. Discuss the pros and cons of mainstreaming students like John and his brother.
7. What could be the real reason the director of human resources changed his mind?
8. What seems to be the director of human resources' prime concern?
9. What are the legal issues involved in this case?
10. Would you contact specific board members and warn them of the up-coming event?

Developing Your Leadership Expertise: ISLLC Standards 2, 4, & 5

Research the law that applies to the rights of students with special needs, and use this information to describe appropriate steps you would take in addressing Mrs. Carlton's complaint.

OUT OF AFRICA A LEADER IS BORN

Eighty-Ninth Street Elementary School with a population of 850 students is located in the Southeast section of a very large school district in a major city that is known for its historic buildings and diverse population. Among the numerous challenges that are faced by the faculty and teachers at 89th Street Elementary is the implementation of the No Child Left Behind Act, which has added to an already difficult situation at the school.

Eighty-Ninth Street Elementary has a student population plagued with gang violence, parents who are either too busy or too absent to care, and a housing project nearby that defies human decency. Given the circumstances, it is remarkable that the teachers manage to teach and the students manage to learn.

Schools similar to 89th Street Elementary School are not extraordinary in America. They are seen on major intersections or tucked away in our alleys and easily ignored by the disinterested and by those who believe they are not affected. Yet, they are places where teachers are faced with the most difficult of daily challenges, student apathy and parent complacency. To not speak of schools in this type of environment is to ignore an integral part of our educational legacy. We created these institutions of learning for our children, but we can easily ignore or neglect the basic needs of the people who teach and work there after we have left.

In spite of the situation at 89th Street Elementary and others like it, there are still lessons to be learned and bits of light that offer hope. In the year 2006, one such story needed to be told; this remarkable tale will serve to remind educators everywhere that, regardless of the situation, there are glimmers of opportunity that exist in schools where you would least expect it.

The Problem

In the school district where Beasley Tunson was employed as a fifth grade teacher, the superintendent approached him and suggested that he should apply for the position of principal for 89th Street Elementary School because the current principal was being reassigned to the middle school. Although Beasley had served as the lead teacher at his current school, he did know if he had the skills to assume a leadership position as a school administrator.

Although Beasley had completed the requirements to become a school administrator more than six years ago, he had always preferred the idea of teaching. He had earned the respect of his colleagues and was known for the many hours he volunteered at a local Boys and Girls Club.

Following an intense search and after Beasley interviewed for the position of principal at 89th Street School, he was offered and accepted the job. The superintendent reminded Beasley that aspiring administrators were encouraged to participate in professional development programs designed to assist aspiring administrators in developing leadership skills.

Beasley chose an internship sponsored by his church as his professional development experience. His assignment would be to travel to Ibadan, Nigeria, where he would help to implement a basic skills curriculum program designed to improve the academic skills of the children in the village of Ibadan.

This enrichment opportunity was offered during the summer months, so it was a perfect professional growth opportunity for Beasley. Beasley submitted his plan to the superintendent, who approved the program and wished Beasley well as he set out across the world in his journey to Nigeria.

Beasley arrived at the small village of Ibadan, Nigeria; what he found when he began his journey was not what he expected. Although he knew that supplies and conditions would be limited, he was surprised to find that not only was there no running water, there was little, if any, water at all. In fact, the villagers walked miles to fetch water from a well and bring it back to the village, only to repeat the ritual the next day. Sometimes the villagers returned without water, and the people were faced with waiting until the next day in hope that water would come.

There were no bathrooms, no desks, no books, no chalk—nothing but an empty room with dirt floors in a place the villagers called school.

On the first day of his assignment, Beasley discovered that there were no other permanent teachers in Ibadan. Instead, teachers came and went. Some teachers came from nearby villages and offered to teach until they were needed back at their own villages; then they returned home, taking with them what few teaching supplies they had brought.

Others who wanted to teach found they had to give up teaching and join with the other villagers in the village infantry to try to protect the village from rebel armies, who were determined to destroy the few remaining homes and take the children away to become part of their warrior mission.

Before Beasley had come to the small village, he had visions of people greeting him and laughing while he played with the children and expectations of speaking to the parents about their hopes and dreams for their children. What he found were children who didn't play and parents who were trying just to survive; many parents had simply disappeared. Even so, the children walked miles to come to school, and with each day came new lessons to learn from a teacher who was there to teach.

Beasley soon learned that the teaching supplies he had brought could be used for better purposes than teaching math and reading. He encouraged the children to sit on the textbooks when he realized that many of them suffered from dysentery and, for sanitary purposes, it was better for the students to avoid sitting on the dirt floors. Education in basic skills was replaced with real-life lessons that were intended to give the children techniques for survival and better health conditions.

Beasley used whatever resources he could draw upon to give the children of Ibadan the most he could in the few weeks remaining of his assignment. He remembered that when he worked with the children in the Boys and Girls Clubs, he would teach them how to avoid gangs and avoid the older students who were determined to recruit them for their street gangs.

Beasley applied the same principles and taught the children how to run and hide from their would-be captors, who would force them to join the rebel army and become part of Africa's "street gangs." It soon became clear to Beasley that although Ibadan and home seemed to be worlds apart, in many ways they became one world united in his heart and for his mission.

The final few weeks in Ibadan passed quickly. On his last day, while Beasley was gathering his belongings, a small boy named Bem, who was one of Beasley's students, came to see him. After visiting with Beasley for a short time and telling him goodbye, Bem reached into his pocket, unfolded a drawing, and handed it to Beasley. Bem said, "Mr. Tunson, this is a gift for you. It is from your students here in Ibadan. It is from us to say thank you for being our teacher. Please take it to America with you and don't forget us."

Beasley said, "Thank you Bem. I will remember you forever." Beasley looked down and saw a drawing of the children and one very tall man. Above the tall man in the picture were the words, "our teacher and our friend."

When Beasley Tunson returned to America and reported to 89th Street School to begin his journey as a first-year principal, he carried with him the drawing that was given to him by Bem. Instead of seeing 89th Street School as an impoverished structure needing paint on the walls and calling for silence in the halls, he heard the voices of children and was reminded of the children in Ibadan. Instead of seeing colors worn by the children as colors worn by gang members, he saw colors of expression and want.

Africa changed Beasley. He no longer looked for signs of defeat that were apparent to outsiders. Instead he looked inside the walls and throughout the halls for promises and possibilities in the faces of the children at 89th Street Elementary School.

This was going to be a very good year, and he would begin a new journey as Beasley Tunson, the educational leader.

Assume for this case that you are an aspiring administrator.

Case Analysis Framework

1. Summarize the case.
2. Identify the problem in a single sentence.
3. Select specific information from the case and categorize it according to people, place, or program.
4. Review and prioritize the information.
5. Refer to the data in each category to solve the problem identified in the case and to respond to the case study questions.

uestions to Research and Consider

1. Do you have schools in your school district that are similar to 89th Street Elementary School? In what way? What are the challenges and solutions?

2. Are teachers and school administrators responsible for the conditions of schools? Why or why not?

3. What can you do as an educator to get more parents involved with the school?

4. In what ways could you motivate children to attend school when the conditions of the school are inadequate?

5. Have you had an experience similar to Beasley Tunson? How has it influenced your role as an educator?

6. How are the conditions in Nigeria similar to conditions in schools in America? Can you think of specific examples?

7. Do you identify with Beasley, and do you believe that effective teachers should aspire to become school leaders? Why or why not?

8. Do you believe that experiences such as Beasley's contribute to school leadership? Why or why not?

9. Can you identify a student that has influenced your role as an educator? How?

10. Have you ever had a life-changing experience that has influenced you as a teacher or school administrator?

Develop Your Leadership Expertise: ISLLC Standards 1, 2, & 3

Identify the steps you would take in designing a curriculum for an impoverished school. Explain how the curriculum would improve the lives of the students.

CAN'T WE WORK THIS OUT?

Oakwood is a rural community located in the Midwest. Parents of school children take pride in Oakwood's schools, and they actively support school events by attending athletic competitions, academic decathlons, and Parent Teacher Organization meetings.

With a population of 6,000 students, the Oakwood Unified School District consists of two elementary schools, one middle school, and one high school. Most of the students have lived in the community all their lives and choose to remain in Oakwood after graduating from high school. An excellent four-year university is located 30 miles outside of town, and it draws its student population from surrounding communities, which represent a diverse population.

Assume for this case that you are the superintendent of the school district.

The Problem

Oakwood High School is a four-year high school with a diverse population of students whose socioeconomic background is primarily blue collar. The teachers enjoy job security, and many of them have worked at the high school for most of their adult lives. It is not unusual for families to meet on weekends for social events in the community and for school teachers to attend with their families.

Recently, the Oakwood High School teachers organized a fundraiser in the spring to aid the parents of a student who was diagnosed with bone marrow cancer. The boy, Tyrone Jackson, was among the most academically talented students in the junior class at the high school. Tyrone had recently been admitted to the honor society at Oakwood High and he was proud of his 4.0 grade point average.

During the same time the spring fundraiser was being held, the governor's office notified all the superintendents of school districts in the state that, due to cuts in the state's budget, all of the districts in the state would be losing funds that had been previously committed. You, the superintendent, had not been forewarned of the budget cuts. At the beginning of the school year, the school board had approved a 5% cost-of-living increase for the following school year for the teachers in your district as part of their new teachers' contract. The decision to award the teachers a 5% increase in salary now coincided with the same school year's budget that will be adversely affected by the budget cuts from the governor's office.

Under your direction, a committee consisting of two district office personnel, one teacher from each school, and the president of the Parent–Teacher Organization was formed to make recommendations to the school board to determine where the cuts in the budget should occur. After taking a serious look at the district's budget, the transportation budget that was once considered a "sacred cow" by the school district and the community was now a topic of discussion. Transportation for students had been provided at no cost to the parents in spite of the fact that costs for transporting students had increased considerably due to rising costs in fuel, replacing and repairing school buses, increasing salaries paid to bus drivers, and the increasing number of buses because of a rise in the student population.

After considerable debate, the members of the committee identified the transportation of students, the funding of after-school athletic programs, and the music program at the elementary schools as areas that should be considered for cost reduction in an effort to balance the budget. You decided to include as a discussion item the committee's recommendations for cost reduction at the next school board meeting.

You never expected what happened next. At the school board meeting, a representative from a small group of parents addressed the school board and proposed using docents to maintain the music program. Next, one of the athletic coaches suggested asking for funds from parents to help defray the cost of the after-school athletic program. These seemed to be reasonable suggestions and you encouraged the school board to consider their suggestions.

However, when the representative from a group of parents, who wished to address the subject of transportation of students, stepped forward, more than 100 parents stood up and began to chant, "We cannot let this happen in Oakwood."

Over the noise of a chanting crowd, Tyrone's father, who represented the angry parents stated, "My name is Mr. Jackson, and I am Tyrone Jackson's father. I have been appointed by the parents and students of Oakwood Unified School District to represent their voice."

He continued, "I would like to address the superintendent, members of the school board, parents, teachers, and district employees. As you know, without the help from the teachers in this district, my son Tyrone would not have received the treatment for his cancer. I will be eternally grateful for the gift of life you have given my son. I am asking you to continue to provide transportation free of charge to the students in this school district. Many of us have spouses who are working outside the home just to put food on our table and to provide a roof over our family's head. Charging money to transport our children to school would be an additional financial burden we cannot bear. We support our teachers, but we know that they have been promised a 5% salary increase for the next year. Can't we work this out?"

Case Analysis Framework
1. Summarize the case.
2. Identify the problem in a single sentence.
3. Select specific information from the case and categorize it according to people, place, or program.
4. Review and prioritize the information.
5. Refer to the data in each category to solve the problem identified in the case and to respond to the case study questions.

Questions to Research and Consider
1. As the superintendent, what is your position regarding the suggestions for consideration for the budget cuts presented by the committee?
2. Do you believe that the governor should be blamed for the budget cuts that have been proposed by her office?
3. Does the school district have the right to challenge the proposed budget cuts from the state?

4. Do you consider transportation of students a right or a privilege?
5. Should the relationship between Mr. Jackson, his son, and the teachers influence your decision regarding how to balance the budget?
6. Whom should you consult with, other than the budget committee, to help establish a strategy for balancing the budget?
7. What information will you need from the state to balance your budget? What relationships between federally and state-funded programs will you need to consider in balancing the budget?
8. Identify alternative ways of providing transportation to students and covering the cost of this service.
9. How would you include school site administrators, parents, students, and other individuals in the final decision regarding the transportation issue?
10. How would you address the 5% cost-of-living increase in salaries for the teachers in the district versus the need to balance the budget? What are the legal and moral considerations?

Developing Your Leadership Expertise: ISLLC Standards 1, 2, 4, & 6

Identify school districts that provide transportation at no cost to the parents of regular education students, charge a minimal fee, or have eliminated student transportation. Present your findings and include in your report your philosophy as it applies to providing transportation to regular education students and its impact on the district's budget, community relations, and the welfare of students.

MISTAKE IN IDENTITY

The Caucasian families who originally moved into the community of Wrongfella formed a strong power base. Since 1975, the population of Wrongfella has become more diverse. Currently, the population is 40% Caucasian, 38% Filipino, 12% Vietnamese, 8% African American, and 2% other. Community and school traditions are challenged as the community's demographics change. Many community members and some staff members at Wrongfella's schools hold onto the past and see a future threatened by the newcomers.

The main campus of Monroe Elementary School was built in 1975. However, it was not constructed to accommodate the increase in enrollment that has occurred over time. Twelve portable classrooms have been added during the past 10 years. The school has 38 teachers, and most of them have been teaching at the school for more than 15 years.

Monroe has approximately 1,200 students, 300 having been identified with limited English-speaking skills. The parents are very supportive of the school, and the parent volunteer program is one of the most active in the school district. The parents helped develop this neighborhood school, and there are strong ties between the school and the parents in the community.

Assume for this case that you are the principal at Monroe Elementary School.

The Problem

At the end of the school day, you are in the process of supervising students. A parent of one of the students at your school approaches you. Mrs. Cast is with her daughter Elise and they are both crying.

Mrs. Cast informs you that something terrible has happened to her daughter, and she insists on meeting with you immediately in your office. You comply with Mrs. Cast's request.

After the three of you enter your office, you invite Mrs. Cast and Elise to be seated. Mrs. Cast tells Elise to share with you what happened to her on the playground during the school day. Elise begins her story by telling you that a boy whose name she thought was Michael was saying dirty things to her during recess and touching her private parts. You ask Elise certain questions so that you can understand clearly what has occurred.

Mrs. Cast responds to your inquiries by accusing you of not supervising the children and allowing terrible things to happen to the children at the school.

You ask Elise if she was certain that it was a boy named Michael from Monroe, and she reassures you that she knows the boy.

At this point you are not convinced that Elise has identified the correct student. The only student named Michael that you are aware of that hangs around the playground during recess is a boy from the nearby junior high school whom you have personally escorted off your campus on more than one occasion.

You question Elise further by asking her to describe the boy. When you inform Mrs. Cast that you believe a junior high school student named Michael and not a student from your school approached her daughter, Mrs. Cast grabs Elise's hand and they abruptly leave your office.

Questions to Research and Consider
1. What will you do next?
2. How will you investigate this matter?
3. Do you believe Elise?
4. What other information do you need to know?

The Investigation

Before you leave work, you decide to telephone Mrs. Cast to inform her that you intend to investigate the matter further. You also apologize for offending her and inform her that you were just trying to do your job. You promise Mrs. Cast that you will notify her as soon as you finish your investigation. You end the conversation by informing Mrs. Cast that you will be out of the office the following day but that you will leave a voice mail for the assistant principal explaining the situation.

You also decide to contact the attendance clerk at the junior high school to inquire about Michael's attendance record at his school. You want to determine whether or not Michael could have been at your school during the school day. The attendance clerk confirms that Michael was reported absent from the junior high school at about the same time Elise reported that the student approached her.

The next day, the vice principal investigates the matter further and speaks with Elise again to confirm the name and description of the student. Elise admits to the vice principal that the student's name was not Michael but Mickey and that he was a fifth-grade student.

The vice principal calls Mickey into the office and instructs him to leave Elise alone and not to treat girls at the school in an inappropriate manner. The vice principal contacts Mrs. Cast with the update and suggests that she meet with you when you return to the campus the next day.

Questions to Research and Consider

1. Are you satisfied with the vice principal's resolution?
2. Would you have done anything differently? If so, what?

The Plot Thickens

On the following day, you meet with the vice principal to compare notes on the details of Elise's case. You are pleased that your assumptions about the student from the junior high school were incorrect. Michael may have been absent from the junior high school, but he had not been at Monroe harassing Elise. The vice principal also informs you that Elise's parents seemed to be satisfied with how he dealt with Mickey.

Three days later, Mickey's mother approaches you at the school and states that she is upset with the manner in which the vice principal interrogated her son. Before you can respond to Mickey's mother, Mrs. Cast walks over to a group of parents and points at Mickey's mother shouting, "Keep your children away from that woman's son!"

Case Analysis Framework

1. Summarize the case.
2. Identify the problem in a single sentence.
3. Select specific information from the case and categorize it according to people, place, or program.
4. Review and prioritize the information.
5. Refer to the data in each category to solve the problem identified in the case and to respond to the case study questions.

Questions to Research and Consider

1. What will you do next?
2. What are the consequences likely to be if you tell the two parents to speak with the vice principal about their concerns?
3. Could this situation have been avoided? If so, how?

Developing Your Leadership Expertise:
ISLLC Standards 1, 3, & 5.

Research the issue of sexual harassment in schools and determine the appropriate steps you should take in addressing the details of this case.

THE COST OF NO CHILD LEFT BEHIND

Mount Claire Elementary School is located in a northwest coastline community of Westvale. Known for its close-knit community and a large population of Chinese immigrants who selected Westvale because of its school's high test scores, Mount Claire is among the state's highest-performing elementary schools. With a population of 900, a minority of the student population is from families who work in the vineyards and are employed as migrant workers. The children from the migrant families are primarily Hispanic, and their parents play a vital role in providing labor for the demands of various wineries in the area.

As part of the No Child Left Behind Act, schools are required to demonstrate that students in specific racial, social, and economic groups are making annual progress. A school might be considered failing if even only one group fails to make progress. When Mount Claire Elementary School plans its annual standardized testing of students, as a compliance factor for No Child Left Behind, it follows a widely accepted practice of seeking permission from the federal government to exclude the test scores of the migrant students. This practice helps the school avoid a penalty that could result if a certain group or groups are not making annual progress.

The Problem

When a new principal, Ms. Monty, was appointed to Mount Claire Elementary School, she decided to challenge the teachers at the school site to include the

Hispanic migrant workers' children in the testing process because she believed that by excluding their scores from the overall scores, the teachers and administration were discriminating against the Hispanic students and not providing the academic instruction they deserved.

The staff reacted by voicing their objection to her ruling. The teachers complained that according to the No Child Left Behind Act, their school would more than likely receive a penalty from the federal government if the scores of the Hispanic students did not reflect annual progress.

Ms. Monty was not convinced that the migrant students' scores should be excluded from the overall scores reported. She continued to insist that the teachers use whatever teaching techniques they saw fit to ensure that the migrant students received equal access to education and an opportunity to demonstrate that they, too, could demonstrate progress on their standardized test scores. After a great deal of convincing, the staff finally agreed to comply with Ms. Monty's suggestion.

In an effort to assist the migrant students in the area of math testing, one of the fifth-grade teachers suggested to the other teachers that migrant students be allowed to use calculators when taking their required annual math tests, which would help the migrant students and make the test less stressful. The first year the migrant students took their math tests, the teacher observed that the students enjoyed using the calculators. The second year, the teachers also allowed the migrant students to use calculators for the annual standardized testing.

When the test scores were submitted for the second year, a federal government employee responsible for evaluating annual test scores and individual school scores noted that Mount Claire had included the scores of the Hispanic migrant students in their reporting and had not asked for permission to omit the scores as they had in the past. The federal employee contacted the school site principal, Ms. Monty, to inquire as to why the migrant students' scores were being included and why the school had not requested permission to exclude the population as they had in the past. Ms. Monty explained her position and informed the federal employee that she was proud that the students had participated in the standardized testing process. The federal employee was suspicious that the test scores were higher than normal for this population of students and wanted to know if the teachers had used any unusual method of testing that could have influenced the test scores and resulted in such a strong gain in test scores.

Ms. Monty followed up the conversation with the federal employee and met with the teachers to determine if, in fact, anything unusual had been done to help the migrant students. During her discussion with the staff, Ms. Monty discovered that the teachers had encouraged the students to use calculators during the math portion of the testing. Even though Ms. Monty had encouraged the teachers to be creative in their teaching methods, she was not aware that the students had used calculators, and she mentioned to the staff that she would have prevented the use of calculators.

The teachers reminded Ms. Monty that the testing experience for the Hispanic migrant students was very difficult, and they thought anything they could do to relieve pressure was a good thing and not necessarily wrong.

After informing the federal employee of the circumstances of the test scores and that the migrant students were allowed to use calculators, a letter from the office of No Child Left Behind Act issued a penalty for Mount Claire Elementary School and notified the school that the scores of the Hispanic migrant students would be excluded. Thus the school would be considered a failing school in this category due to the fact that the test scores would be disqualified because the students were allowed to use calculators while taking their math test.

Ms. Monty met with the staff and informed them of the decision by the federal government. She chose not to chastise her teachers for trying to help the Hispanic migrant students. Instead she asked, "At what cost do we pursue the task of responding to the federal mandates that surround No Child Left Behind? My instructions to you were to include the Hispanic migrant students in the testing process, and this is exactly what you did. Although I was unaware that the students were using calculators—perhaps I should have been more observant—I do not believe that you were meaning to be dishonest. Instead, I believe you were intending to help the students cope with the difficult task of sitting through the tests. I applaud you for your effort and thank you for helping the students. What we are now faced with is the task of dealing with the notion that we are considered a failing school and might lose federal funding. Perhaps it is my fault."

Ms. Monty continued, "But I must ask you again, at what cost do we comply with the No Child Left Behind Act? Is it worth it? Or was it more important to help the migrant students take their tests and know that they tried their best; although they were allowed to use calculators, they were part of the entire learning process when they took the test. No, I believe we did what was right. The No Child Left Behind Act does exactly what it isn't supposed to do.

It encourages us to leave these kids behind because we could have asked permission for them to be excluded under the provisions of the Act."

Ms. Monty added, "I am proud that we did not leave the migrant students behind. Instead we chose to include them, and that was the right thing to do. The migrant education students are just as much a part of us as any group, and I for one am proud that these children attend our school and are important members of our educational family."

Consider for this case that you are a school site principal and not Ms. Monty.

Case Analysis Framework

1. Summarize the case.
2. Identify the problem in a single sentence.
3. Select specific information from the case and categorize it according to people, place, or program.
4. Review and prioritize the information.
5. Refer to the data in each category to solve the problem identified in the case and to respond to the case study questions.

Questions to Research and Consider

1. Do you support the No Child Left Behind Act? Why or why not?
2. Do you believe that schools should be held accountable for test scores of their students?
3. What role should local, state, and federal agencies play in monitoring the progress of student performance in schools?
4. What consequence, if any, should be imposed on schools whose students do not demonstrate that they are learning?
5. Do you believe that standardized tests are the most effective measure of student learning? Why or why not? What other methods would you use to measure student progress? Explain.
6. Do you agree with Ms. Monty and her position that Hispanic migrant students should be included in taking the standardized tests? Why or why not?
7. Would you have supported or not supported the federal government employee's position to penalize the school for allowing the migrant students to use calculators during the math portion of the standardized test?

8. Do you believe that schools should be allowed to exclude certain populations of students' scores when reporting scores to the federal government under the No Child Left Behind Act?

9. Do you believe the No Child Left Behind Act creates an opportunity to discriminate against certain populations of students? If you do, which ones and why?

10. What provisions, if any, would you provide to certain populations of students during the testing process to help them take the standardized tests?

Developing Your Leadership Expertise: ISLLC Standards 2 & 5

Develop a plan for restructuring the No Child Left Behind Act that would allow for all students to be tested for progress in learning without penalties assessed to schools who include all students in the standardized testing process.

AN UNWISE DECISION

Keller Rock Unified School District is located in a rural town in the northeast. The town is situated in the traditional farming community of Ridge Mountain, and some of its younger citizens have been drawn to nearby cities that offer promising jobs and lucrative financial opportunities.

The school district has one high school, one middle school, and two elementary schools. The school board members are extremely supportive of the school and of one another; its members rarely display public disagreement.

School board members usually discover problems in the schools before they are brought to the attention of the superintendent because the community is small and news travels fast.

The most influential parents in the community are known for their familiar relationships with school board members, and it is not uncommon for school board members to find out what is happening in the schools from phone calls at various times during the day, especially from the parents who are most familiar with school board members.

The superintendent has been in his position for only two years. Prior to becoming superintendent, he was the assistant superintendent of the school district, and before that he was the principal of the middle school. He has a reputation as a strict disciplinarian and is very demanding of his staff. The former middle school principal left Keller School District to become an assistant superintendent in a different district.

Assume for this case that you have just been hired as the principal of the middle school. You are new to the school district and to the community.

The Problem

On a Wednesday afternoon during fifth period, you returned to the school site following a meeting at the district office. Your secretary, Ms. Wilson, seems anxious to speak with you. She informs you that she had to locate a teacher at the beginning of fifth period to cover a class for Mr. Brock, one of the school's most popular teachers, because he had not returned to school following lunch.

During the conversation with Ms. Wilson, you learn that Mr. Brock had informed her that he was leaving campus during lunch to return some musical instruments to the local music store and that he would be back to school prior to fifth period.

Ms. Wilson tells you that soon after fifth period began, one of Mr. Brock's students, Kimberly King, came to her office and reported that Mr. Brock had not shown up for his fifth-period class. Kimberly also mentioned that her best friend, Carrie Martin, was absent from Mr. Brock's classroom. Ms. Wilson mentioned that Kimberly seemed very upset that not only was Mr. Brock missing, but so was her best friend.

Kimberly told Ms. Wilson that she knew Carrie was in school that day because they had walked to school together, and they had been in class together during third and fourth periods. Shortly after your conversation with Ms. Wilson, you receive a phone call from Mr. Brock, who is at the local hospital. He informs you that he has been in a traffic accident. He mentions that he was not injured but that one of his students, Carrie Martin, who was with him at the time of the accident, is in serious condition. He adds that the hospital nurse has contacted Carrie's parents and that they are on their way to the hospital.

He explains that he told Ms. Wilson he would return to school prior to fifth period but adds that he knew you would understand why he had not returned because of the traffic accident.

Following your conversation with Mr. Brock and after informing Ms. Wilson that you have learned the whereabouts of Mr. Brock and Carrie, you decide to contact the school district to inform the superintendent of the incident. The superintendent's administrative assistant informs you that the superintendent is at a golf tournament and will not return to the district office until the next morning.

Case Analysis Framework
1. Summarize the case.
2. Identify the problem in a single sentence.
3. Select specific information from the case and categorize it according to people, place, or program.
4. Review and prioritize the information.
5. Refer to the data in each category to solve the problem identified in the case and to respond to the case study questions.

Questions to Research and Consider
1. What do you plan to do next?
2. What are the ethical and legal issues to consider in this case?
3. When the superintendent returns from the golf tournament, what will you tell her?
4. Will you inform Carrie's classmates of her whereabouts?
5. Was it appropriate for Mr. Brock to transport Carrie in his vehicle during lunch period?
6. What will you say to Carrie's parents regarding the situation?
7. If Mr. Brock is found liable for the traffic accident, what will be the school district's liability?
8. How will you address Mr. Brock's behavior when he returns to school?
9. How will you deal with Carrie when she returns to school?
10. Will you leave the school site and visit Carrie at the hospital? Who will you assign to oversee the school in your absence if you decide to go to the hospital?

Developing Your Leadership Expertise:
ISLLC Standards 1, 3, 5, & 6

Plan an in-service training session for your staff that focuses on the rights and responsibilities of teachers who choose to transport students in their private vehicles during and after school hours as well as the legal ramifications of such activities.

LICE AREN'T NICE; PARENTS CAN BE WORSE

Downtown is a community in southern California, which is rich in cultural, racial, and economic diversity. It cherishes its variety of cultural backgrounds and celebrates high expectations for the children who live in Dodgetown. The school district consists of 10 elementary schools, which provide educational services to students in kindergarten through sixth grade.

At Silver Bullet Elementary School, the staff consists of 33 teachers and 13 instructional aides. The population's ethnic distribution includes 43% Caucasian, 30% Hispanic, 14% African American, 2% Native American, 6% Asian, and 5% Pacific Islander students. Silver Bullet is 1 of 10 schools in the district that qualifies for Title I funds, with 94% of the student population qualifying for free or reduced-cost lunches. The school also serves as a center for students with limited English-speaking ability, and it provides instruction to 203 students who are not fluent in English. The parents, administration, and staff are committed to the principle of celebrating life through learning.

For the following case, assume that you are the assistant principal of Silver Bullet Elementary School.

The Problem

On a Monday morning, Starley Night, a first-grade student at Silver Bullet, arrived at the nurse's office for a routine check for head lice. This was becoming a ritual for Starley. Mona, the school nurse, had again found nits in Starley's hair.

Mona telephoned Starley's mom, Ms. Night, and requested that she come to school to pick up her daughter and take care of the problem. When Ms. Night arrived at Mona's office to pick up Starley, she became angry and started yelling at Mona.

You heard the commotion coming from the nurse's office. You approached the parent to calm her down, but you were unsuccessful. Ms. Night informed you that it was the school's fault that her daughter was infested with lice, and she yelled at you and physically assaulted you by striking you on the shoulder. Following this incident, Ms. Night left the school, and you notified the police to report the altercation.

On the following day, Starley returned to school. Not surprisingly, she was still infested with head lice, and Mona knew that the parent had to be contacted. Mona asked you to contact the parent. When you contacted Ms. Night, she was very upset and informed you that she intended to personally contact the school district and file a complaint against Mona and the school district.

Ms. Night called the district office that evening and left a message for the superintendent. She ended her phone call by issuing a bomb threat and stating, "I plan to blow up the whole place and take the school nurse, along with the lice-infested students at Silver Bullet, down with the building."

The superintendent notified the Dodgetown police department after listening to Ms. Night's message. Ms. Night was immediately taken into custody, and, after a brief trial, she was found guilty of a first-offense felony. She was sentenced to 3 months in jail and 90 days of community service.

Three months later, you walked into the teacher's lounge and found Ms. Night working as a volunteer in your school in order to satisfy her community service sentence. To your dismay, the superintendent informed you that you have been assigned to monitor her behavior while she is at your school and fulfilling her community service sentence.

Case Analysis Framework

1. Summarize the case.
2. Identify the problem in a single sentence.
3. Select specific information from the case and categorize it according to people, place, or program.
4. Review and prioritize the information.
5. Refer to the data in each category to solve the problem identified in the case and to respond to the case study questions.

Questions to Research and Consider

1. How do you handle a parent who becomes verbally abusive toward one of your employees?
2. Are parents correct to blame the school for the spread of head lice?
3. What steps should be taken to guarantee that the school is taking all precautions to stop the infestation?
4. What is your reaction to the bomb threat?
5. If Starley returns to school with nits, are you obligated to require Mona to "nit-pick" until all the nits are removed from Starley's hair?
6. Should you distribute information about head lice to all of the parents?
7. Was it appropriate for you to contact the police regarding Ms. Night?
8. Do you agree with the decision to allow Ms. Night to serve her community service sentence at your site? Why or why not?
9. Is it appropriate for Ms. Night to return to your school in the future?
10. What type of relationship should you have with Ms. Night following this incident?

Developing Your Leadership Expertise:
ISLLC Standards 1 & 3

1. Review your school district's policy on head lice.
2. Review your school district's policy on bomb threats.

GOLDEN OLDIES

The community of Vermillion is located in the Midwest. Once a semirural, agricultural town, it is now home to many industrial parks and small corporations. It is quickly becoming a popular family community with several new housing developments under way.

Seven Oaks Elementary School is one of eight elementary schools in the Santa Vista Unified School District, which is located in the heart of Vermillion. It has a population of 950 students. The school was built in 1959, and it is scheduled for a major renovation in the coming year.

The rapid growth of the community has left the school district with no choice other than to implement a four-track, year-round schedule for all its elementary schools. This schedule has served the school community well for the past six years. The community has adjusted to the school calendar, and most of the people agree that it has numerous advantages.

One drawback of the multitrack schedule, however, is that it limits the number of teachers available to teach at certain grade levels. Although the administrators at Seven Oaks Elementary School do not guarantee that a child will be placed in the class of the parent's choice, they do allow parents to submit requests for specific teachers. The district policy states that parent requests are honored as long as the site administrators are able to create classes that are balanced according to the academic ability, ethnicity, and gender of the students at each grade level.

Assume that you are the principal of Seven Oaks Elementary School as you consider this case.

The Problem

Ruby Elliot is a fourth-grade teacher at Seven Oaks. She has taught at the school for the past 28 years, and many of her current students are the children of former students. She has a reputation for being very set in her ways, and the teaching credential that she was awarded 29 years ago does not require her to attend additional courses to maintain her certification.

The administrators at the school site have noticed that her teaching skills have not kept pace with current educational practices, and she does not implement instructional techniques offered at recent school site in-service meetings. Additionally, many parents have criticized Mrs. Elliot's teaching, her overbearing personality, and her loud voice.

In order to help remediate this situation, site administrators provided release time to Mrs. Elliot so she could visit the classrooms of mentor teachers in her district to observe their positive and effective teaching strategies. Mrs. Elliot was also assigned a mentor at her own school site to assist her in developing strategies for improving her curriculum planning and classroom-management skills.

Despite these interventions, there has been no evidence to suggest that Mrs. Elliot has improved her teaching skills. As a consequence, you notified Mrs. Elliot that she will be placed on a yearly evaluation schedule.

Mrs. Elliot was very upset with this decision, and she expressed her disappointment by informing the other teachers that she felt "picked on" and a victim of age discrimination. She reminded the staff that she was obviously a successful teacher and that she had 28 years of experience to prove it!

After four weeks passed, Mrs. Elliot still had not implemented any of the recommendations for improving her teaching style. By the end of the four-track school year, the office had received 44 requests from parents of third graders requesting Mrs. Donaldson, the other fourth-grade teacher assigned to Mrs. Elliot's track, as the teacher of their choice for their child. Only 55 students were enrolled in the third grade, and none of the parents had requested Mrs. Elliot.

Case Analysis Framework

1. Summarize the case.
2. Identify the problem in a single sentence.

3. Select specific information from the case and categorize it according to people, place, or program.
4. Review and prioritize the information.
5. Refer to the data in each category to solve the problem identified in the case and to respond to the case study questions.

Questions to Research and Consider

1. What are the most important issues involved in this case?
2. What issue needs to be resolved first? Second? Third?
3. Do you inform the individual in charge of personnel at your district office of this situation? Why or why not?
4. What criteria should you use in placing the fourth-grade students in classes for the next four-track year?
5. What is your opinion of the policy that honors parents' requests for teachers?
6. Would you review all Mrs. Elliot's formal evaluations before deciding what action to take?
7. What steps can you take as an administrator to require Mrs. Elliot to implement the suggestions aimed at improving her teaching?
8. What recourse do you have if she continues to ignore your recommendations?
9. How do you address the fact that Mrs. Elliot has tenure as a teacher?
10. How will you monitor Mrs. Elliot in the future?

Developing Your Leadership Expertise: ISLLC Standards 2 & 6

Research the law in your state as it relates to teacher tenure, and explain how it would influence the administrator's role in evaluating Mrs. Elliot. If your state does not award teachers tenure, explain how Mrs. Elliot's employment status might be affected by her behavior.

VOUCHER AS THE VOICE OF THE PEOPLE

T he inner-city housing project in Templeton has been condemned, and the city council is considering a proposal to build a new low-income housing development. Local gangs have staked out their territory, and it is very clear to everyone in Templeton who rules what corner and for how long. The line drawn between racial boundaries is distinct and well defined by the teens that rival with their peers to dominate Templeton's turf.

Because the state approved a voucher program that would award funds to low-income families so they could choose to send their children to private schools, the school board has decided to list this subject as one of the discussion items at the next school board meeting.

The superintendent and the school board are not concerned about students leaving 54th Street High School. Even though it is the only public high school in Templeton, there have been only a handful of parents who are disgruntled. Additionally, the district is convinced that the parents will not use vouchers to send their children to the only other high school in the area, which is a private Catholic high school, St. John's.

Assume for this case that you work at the district office and have been appointed by the superintendent to meet with a group of dissatisfied parents.

The Problem

Harry Bee is a graduate of 54th Street High School and a businessperson in the area who launched an aggressive campaign to support the state's voucher system. He has personally accepted credit for the passage of the ballot initiative. He boasts on a regular basis that the only thing he ever received from his experience at 54th Street High School was the opportunity to skip afternoon classes so he could hang out with his buddies and drink beer. Fortunately, Harry turned his life around, and, after graduating from high school, he developed a software program that legalized E-commerce gambling. The rest is history.

After the voters approved the voucher system in his district and, subsequently, in the state, Harry left Templeton with his childhood sweetheart Vickie Lou and moved to Chicago.

During the past five years, while big-mouth Harry Bee was bragging about his accomplishments, Wilma Max and her friends were developing a list of concerns to take to the local school board that addressed what they believed were critical problems at the high school. They informed the school board that they wanted safer schools, improved academic programs, and better leadership.

Mr. Bruno, the principal of 54th Street High School, informed the school board that, in spite of Wilma's concerns, he believed that the parents of the 54th Street High School students were too busy finding jobs, feeding themselves, and keeping track of their children to pay attention to how the district does its job.

The school board agreed with Mr. Bruno and ignored the complaints. They dismissed Wilma's concerns and those of her friends, considering them nosy zealots who had nothing better to do than to stick their noses in the business of people who knew what they were doing.

After Wilma left the first school board meeting, she formed a group called "In My Backyard" (IMBY). The group grew from 10 to 75 members, and within three years the IMBYs were meeting on a regular basis on behalf of their neighborhood and their schools.

Meanwhile, Mr. Bruno agreed to meet with Wilma's group on a semiregular basis, but nothing ever came of the meetings except Mr. Bruno's comment, "Thank you, ladies, for coming. See you soon."

The IMBYs decided that they had had enough of the school board, the superintendent, and the 54th Street High School principal. They began a campaign to promote St. John's High School and encouraged parents in the neighborhood to use their vouchers to pay tuition to St. John's.

When the next school year began, the enrollment at 54th Street High School dropped by 250 students, and the enrollment at St. John's increased by about the same amount.

You have been instructed by the superintendent to meet with the IMBYs.

Case Analysis Framework

1. Summarize the case.
2. Identify the problem in a single sentence.
3. Select specific information from the case and categorize it according to people, place, or program.
4. Review and prioritize the information.
5. Refer to the data in each category to solve the problem identified in the case and to respond to the case study questions.

Questions to Research and Consider

1. Do you need to develop a relationship with Wilma and her friends?
2. What information do you take back to the superintendent and the board?
3. How will you gather data from the IMBYs that will prove beneficial in developing a plan to keep the parents from sending their children to St. John's?
4. What other individuals will you speak to regarding your assignment?
5. How will you advise the school board on this matter?
6. What impact could the voucher program have on the school district?
7. What can you do to put an end to the declining enrollment?
8. Will you develop a relationship with the administrators at St. John's? Why or why not?
9. What do you plan to do if the voucher system develops further to include additional families in the area?
10. Do you believe that Mr. Bruno handled the concerns of the community appropriately? Why or why not?

Developing Your Leadership Expertise: ISLLC Standards 1, 2, 4, & 5

1. Develop a strategic plan to address the issue of the voucher program and its impact.
2. Develop a plan for your school that focuses on marketing your school to parents who have a choice between public and private school placement.

TO BE OR NOT TO BE THE SUBSTITUTE

The community of Alexandria is populated with individuals who are highly educated and quite wealthy. Most of the mothers do not work outside of the home, and they volunteer at the school on a regular basis. The families value education and want to be involved in the educational process. Almost all the parents could send their children to a private school, but they are committed to making their public school the very best that it can be.

Emerson Elementary School opened five years ago, and its current enrollment is 425 students, with an ethnically balanced student population. The staff are extremely close with one another and are quite talented. The teachers, administrator, and parents at Emerson are committed to working together to meet the needs of the students.

For this situation, assume that you are the principal at Emerson.

The Problem

You were appointed three years ago to take the place of a highly respected principal. You are a young female and served as a classroom teacher at Emerson prior to becoming an administrator. The majority of the staff and parents supported your appointment to this position. A recent survey confirmed this fact and revealed that these groups believe that you make decisions based on what you believe is best for the children.

One of the third-grade teachers at your school, Ms. Jeffrey, has just been diagnosed with breast cancer. She meets with you and explains that she is scheduled to have surgery next week and will begin receiving radiation treatment directly following the surgery. She shares with you the fact that she will undergo chemotherapy at a later time as part of her treatment plan. The two of you discuss her teaching options and decide that it would be best for her and her students if she were to take a medical leave and arrange for a substitute teacher to finish the school year with her students.

You and Ms. Jeffrey decide that the perfect person for the job is a substitute teacher who has just finished a long-term third-grade teaching assignment at another school in the district. Additionally, this teacher, Ms. Murphy, substituted for Ms. Jeffrey three years ago when she was on maternity leave. Ms. Murphy is familiar with the curriculum and the school routine. Ms. Jeffrey mentions to you that Ms. Murphy is the aunt of one of her students, but she states that she is confident that this will not present a problem. You inform Ms. Jeffrey that you intend to share with the parents of her students the fact that she is leaving and that Ms. Murphy will be serving as the substitute teacher.

That same afternoon, you call Ms. Murphy and schedule an appointment with her to discuss the possibility of her substituting for Ms. Jeffrey. During the meeting you mention that you are aware that her nephew is enrolled in Ms. Jeffrey's class and ask her if she thinks this will be a problem. She assures you that not only will it not be a problem, but that she is looking forward to teaching her nephew in Ms. Jeffrey's class. You tell Ms. Murphy that she is a strong candidate and that you will contact her the following day if you decide to offer her the position.

Following lunch, you return to your office and discover that there is a message from the mother of Ms. Murphy's nephew. She requests that you call her immediately.

You contact the parent, and she informs you that she is very upset because the school is considering hiring her sister-in-law to teach her son's class. You are obviously surprised that she has heard about the possibility of this happening, and you ask her to share with you how she learned the news. You also invite her to tell you what concerns she has regarding the matter.

She explains to you that Ms. Murphy had already informed another relative back east that she was interviewing for the substitute position. She informs you that her family has taken drastic steps, including moving across the country, to break away from their relatives back east. It appears from everything you can gather that she has no quarrel specifically with the sister-in-law, Ms. Murphy, but she is quite concerned that Ms. Murphy might share information with other family members regarding her son and his family. She wants to know if you plan to hire Ms. Murphy.

Case Analysis Framework
1. Summarize the case.
2. Identify the problem in a single sentence.
3. Select specific information from the case and categorize it according to people, place, or program.
4. Review and prioritize the information.
5. Refer to the data in each category to solve the problem identified in the case and to respond to the case study questions.

Questions to Research and Consider
1. How do you respond to the parent?
2. How much weight do you give the mother's concerns?
3. Should parents be involved in the process of hiring substitute teachers?
4. What additional information will you need prior to making a decision?
5. Should you speak to the nephew regarding hiring his aunt?
6. If you believe that Ms. Murphy is the best candidate for the job, do you disregard the parent's concerns?
7. If you decide to hire Ms. Murphy, what options could you offer to the parent?
8. Should you speak with the substitute regarding the mother's concerns?
9. What are the possible ramifications of hiring Ms. Murphy?
10. What are the possible ramifications of not hiring Ms. Murphy?

Developing Your Leadership Expertise: ISLLC Standards 2 & 6

> Research your district's policy regarding hiring relatives of students. Identify positive and negative consequences of hiring relatives of students.

MRS. BUMBLE AND HER BAND OF BUSYBODIES

St. Petersburg has relied on federal funds to subsidize the majority of its programs for students who qualify for federal assistance. One initiative that has been introduced to the largest school district in the city is the computer lab, which provides 60 computer stations and one instructor. Other programs include the free and reduced-cost lunch and breakfast programs provided to students each school day.

The community is proud of its students and has successfully applied for and received grants from the National Science Foundation (NSF), the Montgomery League, and the local chapter of the Woman's Democratic Caucus.

In close proximity to St. Petersburg is the small but rather influential community of Dunsberry, which happens to have as one of its distinguished residents the governor of the state. The majority of Dunsberry's citizens have lobbied for years to convince the governor to take the message of local control of federal funds to the federal level.

Recently, the federal government recommended and approved a program that allows individual states to decide on how to use some of the federal funds. The initiative lifted the federal restrictions attached to federal funding and allowed states more leniency in how federal funds are spent to provide educational programs and services to students enrolled in public schools.

The Dunsberry Unified School District was pleased to hear of this initiative, whereas the St. Petersburg community feared the consequences of the federal government's decision.

Assume for this case that you are the principal in Dunsberry.

The Problem

For many years Dunsberry and St. Petersburg have remained distant cousins. The conservative environment of Dunsberry and the liberal atmosphere of St. Petersburg have divided the communities and the school districts.

When the citizens of Dunsberry heard about the federal government's intention to allow states to decide the best use of federal funds, they immediately formed an advisory committee. The purpose of this group was to convince the school district's elementary school principal to stop providing free and reduced-cost lunches to the students who qualified for it under the federal assistance program. The committee was chaired by Mrs. Bumble.

The members of the advisory committee were parents from the community who believed that it was not the government's responsibility to feed students but rather it was the responsibility of the parents. They were convinced that instead of using the money to feed students, they could use the funds to build a computer lab just like the one that St. Petersburg had in its school district.

The first item on the Dunsberry Advisory Committee's agenda was to meet with you and lobby for their position. At the meeting, you explained to the group your understanding of the federal government's position on the subject.

You informed the advisory committee members that, although the federal government had removed some of its control over certain categories, it had no intention of turning over the free and reduced-cost lunch program to the states. You explained that the federal government was clear from the beginning that funds that would be used to provide food to students were not to be interfered with and that students who qualified for the program were to continue to receive their lunches at the federal government's expense.

You added that you would not end the program even if you could because you could see the benefit of the program for the students. You made the recommendation to Mrs. Bumble and her advisory committee that the school would be better served if the committee focused on curriculum matters and left the nourishment of students to the government.

Mrs. Bumble was not pleased with your response to the committee's inquiry, so she decided to take the matter to a higher level. The next day she contacted the governor's office and set up an appointment with him. Considering that the governor was Mrs. Bumble's neighbor and that her husband had played golf with him just last week, this was not a difficult meeting to arrange.

At the meeting, Mrs. Bumble shared her concern about the federal government's role in feeding students and informed the governor that she represented a very influential group of parents who shared her concern. She encouraged the governor to take the matter directly to the federal government officials. She added as she left his office that he should also speak with Dunsberry's superintendent and recommend that you be fired.

Case Analysis Framework

1. Summarize the case.
2. Identify the problem in a single sentence.
3. Select specific information from the case and categorize it according to people, place, or program.
4. Review and prioritize the information.
5. Refer to the data in each category to solve the problem identified in the case and to respond to the case study questions.

Questions to Research and Consider

1. As the elementary school principal, what is your role in deciding the distribution of federal funds at your school?
2. Do you believe you handled the meeting with the advisory committee in a constructive manner?
3. What would you have done differently?
4. Would you contact the superintendent regarding this matter?
5. What are your concerns, given the fact that Mrs. Bumble is on friendly terms with the governor?
6. What is your position regarding the state control of federal funds?
7. Do you believe that the federal government should have less jurisdiction over some of the federally funded programs? If so, which ones?
8. How would you react if the federal government stopped providing funds for free and reduced-cost lunches to students in the public school system?

9. Do you believe this program has an influence on the students' ability to achieve in school?
10. As the principal, do you believe it is appropriate to discuss political topics such as federal versus state funding of school programs with the parents of the students at your school?

Developing Your Leadership Expertise: ISLLC Standards 2, 3, & 5

Write a position paper on the use of power by special interest groups and on how it influences the role of school administrators.

CAUGHT IN THE WEB

The Midwestern town of Benton is nestled among low-lying hills. The people who live in this secluded area often refer to themselves as the "keepers of the dream." They have managed to preserve their past and create a cultural boundary around the town that serves as a gatekeeper to prevent the influx of high technology and new-wave discoveries that they believe could threaten the serenity of the town.

The population reflects a balanced ethnic blend of people who work well together. The community is respected for its work ethic, and the local people take pride in owning their own land. Some of the Hispanic citizens of Benton have owned land for more than 100 years, and their families maintain the land and produce wonderful crops.

Assume for this case that you are the principal of Benton High School.

The Problem

The Cruz family members are among the wealthiest Hispanic landowners. They have resided in Benton for more than 100 years. They own their land, produce bountiful crops, and have instilled in generations of children the value of learning and a respect for their heritage.

The oldest of the Cruz children is Helena, a junior in high school with a grade point average of 3.8. She is interested in composing music and hopes to obtain a scholarship and attend college.

Benton High School is the only high school in the area. There are three elementary schools and one middle school in the school district. The current high school enrollment is 523 students, and the focus of the curriculum is on language arts and math. The largest organization at the high school is the Future Farmers of America. New to Benton High School is a computer lab, which was donated by a former alumnus who graduated from the school in 1948. She designated $80,000 in her will for building a computer lab.

Helena was excited about the new lab. She knew that in order to secure a scholarship for the university she would need technology skills and a computer class on her transcript. Even though she had a computer in her room at home, she wanted to use the lab at school to write her papers and conduct research on the Internet.

You have been serving as the only administrator at the high school for the past five years. Prior to that, a teacher was assigned as the lead teacher in charge to manage most of the school affairs. You were not pleased about the construction of the new lab facility. You felt that the introduction of technology to your small campus would interfere with the curriculum already established by the teachers. Nonetheless, you accepted the donation and agreed with the school board to support the construction and implementation of a technology program at Benton High. You assigned one of the math teachers, Ms. Calmly, to supervise the lab and wished her well in developing the program. You informed her that unless there was a major problem, you would prefer that she take care of all the computer lab affairs.

Ms. Calmly set up the computer lab and recruited a few parent volunteers to assist the students. She appointed one of her most enthusiastic students, Helena, to be in charge of helping other students learn the technology.

One of the first projects Ms. Calmly assigned her students was to develop a Web page. She considered this a safe assignment and thought that it would take her students at least a semester to develop the Web page and post it on the Internet.

Of course, she underestimated Helena's interest in promoting the use of the technology. Within two weeks Helena had developed a Web page. She decided that because no one else at the school was familiar with the Internet, she would post her Web page herself. In order to promote her school, Helena posted one of the weekly bulletins that you mailed home to the parents of the high school students.

Helena failed to read the entire bulletin before posting it. At the bottom was a message from you. You wrote, "We are in dire need of musical instruments and cannot hold our seasonal holiday play this year without more instruments. Please deliver any musical instruments that you no longer need to the school office as soon as possible. There is no need to call."

By Monday morning of the following week, Helena was receiving messages on her Web page inquiring about the request for donations of musical instruments. These inquiries were coming from all over the world. In addition, the school office had received 53 phone calls and 10 letters asking for information about the solicitation. Within six weeks, total strangers had donated 62 flutes, 16 French horns, 7 trombones, and 5 guitars to Benton's music department and the Salvation Army had personally delivered 9 sets of used drums.

Case Analysis Framework
1. Summarize the case.
2. Identify the problem in a single sentence.
3. Select specific information from the case and categorize it according to people, place, or program.
4. Review and prioritize the information.
5. Refer to the data in each category to solve the problem identified in the case and to respond to the case study questions.

Questions to Research and Consider
1. How are you going to handle the situation with Helena?
2. What steps will you take in dealing with Ms. Calmly?
3. What plans do you have for the musical instruments that are on their way to Benton?
4. What can you do to stop the musical instruments from coming to Benton?
5. What will change, if anything, in the way you communicate with your staff in the future?
6. What will you tell the school board?
7. How can you turn this into a positive experience?
8. What influence, if any, do you think the posting of the Web page on the Internet will have on the town of Benton?

9. What will you do with the nine sets of used drums from the Salvation Army?

10. How do you intend to involve Helena's parents?

Developing Your Leadership Expertise: ISLLC Standards 1, 2, & 4

Locate Web pages on the Internet that feature individual schools and school districts, and identify what you believe is the primary focus of the Web site for each one you visit.

THE BIBLE AND MS. WRIGHT

Laurel Palm Middle School has a reputation as one of the most successful schools in Dayton. For the last three years, the school has been awarded a National Distinguished School Award, and it has been identified by the state as one of the top 10 performing schools. With a population of 1,500 students and a multicultural student body, the administration, teachers, and students have been recognized for their united front in celebrating teaching and learning and inviting parents to play an active role in planning school programs and improving all aspects of the school and its operations.

Nestled between the Jonathan Ode Community Cultural Center, named after the city's founder, and the high school and recognized for its high percentage of students attending four-year universities following graduation, Laurel Palm Middle School was considered a model school.

The Problem

Ms. Eleanor Avery, the principal of Laurel Palm Middle School, has a reputation for leading her staff with an innovative and supportive style that motivates the faculty and creates an environment where new ideas are encouraged and innovative programs are supported. She has served as a school administrator for over a decade and she has the support of her teachers, parents, and students.

Each school year, Ms Avery establishes specific curriculum goals and objectives that align with the school district. In addition, she has formed a school site committee that she has charged with developing new and interesting curriculum programs.

In the past the committee has been successful and has proposed new ideas, such as improving the science curriculum and developing a continuum for learning in math and literature. In each case, the district has supported the programs and, with minor changes, adopted the programs districtwide for the middle schools in the school district.

For the current school year, one of the parents on the committee, Ms. Beckel, made the suggestion that a religious studies course would be an interesting addition to the current curriculum program. She had learned that other schools in various campuses throughout the state were including courses on religion in their curriculum, and she received support from the rest of the committee, including Ms. Avery.

Ms. Beckel and Ms. Kassidy, a classroom teacher who also served on the committee, were planning on presenting the new religious studies course at the next school site meeting after they had included suggestions from all the committee members and prepared the final document. Included in the program proposal was a textbook recommendation that listed the Bible as one of the references to be used for the religious studies course.

Prior to the school site meeting where the new religious studies curriculum program was to be formally presented to the school site committee, Ms. Beckel invited her neighbor, Ms. Wright, to her home for coffee. During the visit, Ms. Wright learned from Ms. Beckel about the upcoming plans to present the religious studies curriculum, including using the Bible as one of the texts for the course.

Ms. Wright had no children of her own, but she always showed an interest in Ms. Beckel's involvement with the middle school. Over the years, Ms. Wright had even elected to volunteer at Laurel Palm Middle School's annual fund-raising events.

As Ms. Beckel and Ms. Wright concluded their conversation, Ms. Wright said, "You know I have been a supporter of the middle school, and I have even volunteered to help at the annual fund-raisers over the years, and I consider you my friend, but if you think that I will stand by and let you and your committee introduce the Bible as a textbook, you are mistaken. I have always believed in separation of church and state, and this idea crosses a boundary. And I for one will not support it."

Ms. Beckel was surprised by Ms. Wright's reaction. She replied, "I don't understand your comment. The Bible is a piece of literature that clearly explains the foundation of a belief of one religion. The religious studies program is going to include numerous religious references, including the Koran. What is the big deal?"

Ms. Wright left Ms. Beckel's home and offered the following response, "You have not heard the end of this. I have known you for many years and I have not shared my personal views on this topic because there was no need, but you must know that even though we are friends, I will not stand by and see this type of curriculum introduced in the school—and especially the use of the Bible." With that said, Ms. Wright left.

Ms. Beckel assumed that even though Ms. Wright was upset, she would not hear from her again on the subject. This was to be the first of many assumptions that Ms. Beckel would make that would prove to be wrong.

The following week, at the school site meeting, Ms. Beckel and Ms. Kassidy presented the religious studies curriculum program to Ms. Avery and the committee. Ms. Avery accepted the program proposal and planned on presenting the proposal at the next school board meeting, which was scheduled for the following week.

When Ms. Avery, Ms. Beckel, and Ms. Kassidy arrived at the school board meeting the following week to make their presentation, there to greet them were the local media and Ms. Wright, who was waving a large sign that read, "Save our children. Separate church from state. Save the Constitution."

Assume for this case that you are Ms. Avery, the principal of Laurel Palm Middle School.

Case Analysis Framework

1. Summarize the case.
2. Identify the problem in a single sentence.
3. Select specific information from the case and categorize it according to people, place, or program.
4. Review and prioritize the information.
5. Refer to the data in each category to solve the problem identified in the case and to respond to the case study questions.

Questions to Research and Consider

1. As the school site principal, do you believe that a committee of parents and teachers is qualified to develop curriculum programs for the school? Why or why not?

2. Should Ms. Beckel have told you that her neighbor reacted as she did with the news about using the Bible as a reference for the course? What would you have done if you would have found out?

3. Do you believe that Ms. Wright has a right to her opinion? Why or why not?

4. What would you have done when you arrived at the school board meeting and were met by Ms. Wright and the media?

5. Do you believe as the school principal you were obligated to inform the superintendent of the details of the curriculum program prior to the school board meeting? Should you have informed anyone else other than the superintendent at the school district?

6. As the principal, what could you have done to avoid the scene at the school board meeting?

7. What precautions if any, would you have taken to discourage the media from attending the meeting?

8. What documents, if any, would you refer to that would justify using the Bible as a reference for the religious studies course?

9. What would you do in the future to work with the committee to make certain that this type of incident would not happen again?

10. Do you believe that your reputation as an excellent school administrator would help you to persuade the school board to implement the religious studies course including using the Bible as one of the texts?

Developing Your Leadership Expertise: ISLLC Standards 5 & 6

Research the subject of separation of church and state as it applies to school curricula and write a position paper to support or reject the use of the Bible in school as a reference text for a religious studies course. Be prepared to defend your position.

TOLERANCE TEST FOR RANCHO

The city of Carterville was known for its magnolia tree–lined streets and its old Victorian houses. Single families who moved to the area were committed to restoring the older homes and preserving the charm of the community. The downtown section of town was known as *Littletown* to the locals and tourists, who realized that novelty shops and antique malls provided an atmosphere of nostalgia and an opportunity for unique purchases.

Many of the families who lived in Carterville were churchgoing folks who valued the ideas of the "stay-at-home mom" and weekend family outings. Although the socioeconomic conditions created an illusion that most of the families could afford to have one parent working, many families struggled to make ends meet, and often stay-at-home moms found that creating home businesses provided the additional income needed to balance the family budget.

Assume for this case that you are the new principal of Rancho Elementary School.

The Problem

Carterville Unified School District was located in the center of town. Drawing its student population from areas outside of Carterville, the school district was composed of various ethnic groups from diverse socioeconomic backgrounds at every grade level. Parents living in Littletown enrolled their children in

Rancho Elementary School and considered Rancho to be the best elementary school in the district.

Under the direction of the district superintendent and school board, the school district adopted a zero-tolerance policy that applied to all of the schools in the district. The policy included zero tolerance for truancies from school, for weapons of any kind, for physical assaults, and for sexual harassment.

The district's superintendent advised all the site administrators in the district to include the zero-tolerance policy in their respective school plans. He directed principals at each school site to distribute copies of the revised school plans to the parents of every student at each school site.

As the principal of Rancho Elementary, you appointed one of the fifth-grade teachers, Ms. Idleman, to be in charge of developing the school plan. She was one of the lead teachers at the school, and she had just completed a program that qualified her to become a school administrator. You reminded her to include the zero-tolerance policy in the school plan, although it was your opinion that students at Rancho Elementary would not be inclined to violate the zero-tolerance policy.

On the day Ms. Idleman's committee completed the school plan and forwarded it to your office for approval, you were attending a conference away from school. In your absence, Ms. Boxer, the assistant principal, who was a tenured employee in the district, was in charge. She served on the school plan committee that Ms. Idleman chaired.

On the same day you were absent, your administrative assistant informed Ms. Boxer that the school plan had been completed and that it had been forwarded to your office for approval. Ms. Boxer was confident that the document would meet with your approval and approved the plan in your absence. She instructed the school clerk to duplicate the school plan and send a copy home with each one of the students at the end of the school day.

A few days later, Ms. Idleman was teaching a unit to her students that focused on historical structures in Littletown. She developed a lesson plan that required the students to conduct research on Littletown and prepare reports that were to be presented to the class.

Becky Skutter was the last student to present her report to the class. Following her presentation, Becky reached for a paper bag that she had brought with her and removed what looked like an old handgun. She informed the class that her father had found the item in the attic when he was renovating their Victorian home. Becky's father believed the pistol was from the 19th century and was brought over from England at the turn of the century.

When Ms. Idleman saw the pistol, she quietly instructed Becky to place the item back in the paper bag and hand it over to her. Ms. Idleman informed Becky that she would return the handgun to her at the end of the school day. As promised, Ms. Idleman returned the pistol to Becky and instructed her to keep the pistol in the paper bag and return it to her father. Becky received an "A" grade for her report.

On the following day, one of the parents of a student in Ms. Idleman's class contacted you and demanded that something be done with the student who brought the gun to school. The parent was angry and said that she planned to contact the superintendent, the local newspaper, and other parents of the children in Ms. Idleman's class to see if any of the other children had nightmares like her daughter had after seeing the weapon at school.

Case Analysis Framework

1. Summarize the case.
2. Identify the problem in a single sentence.
3. Select specific information from the case and categorize it according to people, place, or program.
4. Review and prioritize the information.
5. Refer to the data in each category to solve the problem identified in the case and to respond to the case study questions.

Questions to Research and Consider

1. How would you respond to the parent who contacted you and was angry about the handgun?
2. Would you hold Ms. Boxer responsible for approving the school plan that included the zero-tolerance policy without your final approval?
3. What steps would you take in determining whether or not Becky or her parents were aware of the zero-tolerance policy?
4. Do you consider the fact that Becky brought the pistol to school to be in violation of the zero-tolerance policy?
5. What program can you implement to ensure that every parent of every child in your school is familiar with the zero-tolerance policy?
6. What questions will you ask Ms. Boxer and Ms. Idleman?

7. Should Becky be suspended from school? Who should you consult, if anyone, before you make the decision?
8. What consequences, if any, should Ms. Idleman receive for not reporting that Becky had brought the handgun to school?
9. What steps would you take to communicate with the parents of other children in Ms. Idleman's class regarding the handgun incident?
10. Do you believe this incident will change the way people view your school?

Developing Your Leadership Expertise: ISLLC Standard 3

Conduct an Internet search and identify school districts that implement zero-tolerance policies. Compare the policies in terms of the language, due process, and consequences for violating zero-tolerance policies.

CULTURAL CLASH AND CURRICULUM CHAOS

Sun Coast Unified School District is a medium-sized, suburban school district with an enrollment of 13,000 students. Some schools are composed mostly of children from very low income families, whereas other schools consist of families from the upper middle class. The diverse community houses the district's 13 elementary schools, 4 middle schools, 2 comprehensive high schools, and 1 charter school.

The Educational Services Department at the district office is responsible for curriculum, staff development, and all the categorical programs. The staff consists of an associate superintendent; an assistant superintendent of instruction; a director of special education; a director of student services; and four coordinators responsible for curriculum, assessment, and categorical programs.

The district has been featured in the media recently because of a proposed bond measure that would provide funding for building additional schools to facilitate the increasing number of students who are moving into the community, most of whom are Spanish speaking. If the bond passes, three new schools will be built and many of the older ones will be modernized. Without the passage of the bond measure, the district will face severe problems with overcrowding and substandard facilities.

The English Language Learner (ELL) population of students continues to grow. Within two years the district expects that 35% of the students will qualify for programs designed to meet the needs of the ELL students.

For this case, assume that you are the director of student services and in charge of the bilingual program for the Sun Coast Unified School District.

The Problem

A law was just passed in the state that calls for an end to bilingual education. The passage of this law has been met with support as well as protest from various segments of the community. Currently, Sun Coast Unified School District has a bilingual program at every campus, and the district strongly supports primary language development programs. With the passage of the new legislation, the district is faced with the challenge of following the guidelines set down by the law and at the same time maintaining its commitment to the needs of its bilingual student population.

Adding to the problem, the law has been interpreted differently by various school districts in the state, and a uniform policy regarding bilingual education is clearly absent. Sun Coast Unified School District received a great deal of criticism for its interpretation of the law, primarily from the English-speaking population in the community, who demanded that the district adhere to the law by ending bilingual education. This same constituency resents the idea that more schools need to be built to accommodate the Spanish-speaking newcomers.

In contrast to this group, a growing number of Spanish-speaking parents want the school district to continue to provide bilingual education for their children. The school district has a reputation for meeting the needs of its Spanish-speaking students; for many of the parents, this is the reason they moved to the area and enrolled their children in the district's schools.

To further complicate matters, the superintendent of the school district supports the bilingual program, but her husband, who is a classroom teacher in one of the district's elementary schools, does not. In fact, he was overheard at a recent school meeting stating that he strongly believed that the Spanish-speaking students did not need bilingual education and that they would perform better in school without the program.

Recently, you heard a rumor from one of the more vocal parents in the community that a large group of parents were planning to attend the next school board meeting. According to the rumor, representatives from both sides of the bilingual debate intend to share their opinions with the school board about how the district should respond to the passage of the new law. Each group wants to know how the new legislation will affect their children's education.

Case Analysis Framework

1. Summarize the case.
2. Identify the problem in a single sentence.
3. Select specific information from the case and categorize it according to people, place, or program.
4. Review and prioritize the information.
5. Refer to the data in each category to solve the problem identified in the case and to respond to the case study questions.

Questions to Research and Consider

1. If the rumor proves to be true, how do you prepare for this meeting?
2. What additional information do you need?
3. What are some things you could do to promote the involvement of the parents whose primary language is not English?
4. There are a few classroom teachers who do not support the district's bilingual program. How do you respond to their lack of support for the program?
5. What steps can you take in educating the English-speaking community concerning bilingual education?
6. What should be the role of the superintendent regarding the district's bilingual education program?
7. A parent advocate for bilingual education brings a flyer to your office and hands it to you. It is an invitation to parents who are interested in promoting the bilingual educational program to attend a meeting to develop a strategy for promoting their cause. How would you react? What would you do?
8. The superintendent contacts you and wants to meet with you within a week regarding the status of the bilingual program. How do you prepare for the meeting with her?
9. A principal from one of the schools in the district informs you that a group of Spanish-speaking parents have met with him to request that a committee be formed to address their concerns regarding the bilingual educational program at his school. How do you respond to his message?
10. What information will you provide to the parents who want to know how the recent legislation to end bilingual education will affect their children?

Developing Your Leadership Expertise:
ISLLC Standards 1, 5, & 6

Develop a plan for working with parents at your school who have opposing viewpoints regarding bilingual education.

RECLAIMING ROSE PLACE

Rose Place is a middle-class community that has been engaged in the development of a new low-income housing project. During the past 50 years, it has been the home of influential white supremacists. This group frequently protests changes in the community and has recently voiced dissatisfaction with the low-income housing project. They have expressed concern about the potential problems they believe newcomers will bring to the area.

Even though it was believed that many of the original white supremacy members migrated to regions elsewhere in the nation, they left behind many children and grandchildren who have been influenced by their ancestors.

Smith-Jackson is a 40-year-old elementary school located just north of the center of town. It has an enrollment of 600 students, 20 of whom are special-needs students who require classrooms with special access to accommodate their physical handicaps. The community is proud of this program, and many of the parents in the area volunteer to help the physically handicapped students at Smith-Jackson.

In addition to these students who are bused to the elementary school, the school district has adopted a voluntary busing program that encourages underrepresented students to enroll in the school. This is the district's attempt to integrate Smith-Jackson in response to the state's mandate that all schools be integrated by the end of the decade.

In spite of the community's acceptance of the busing program that brings special education students to Rose Place, there is a strong and vocal group of parents who object to the busing of students to the elementary school who are ethnically different from the majority of the population in the community. According to some individuals, "If they aren't white, they aren't right." This same group of parents is quick to point out to the school board that a number of the students who participate in the voluntary busing program are experiencing problems at school and do not seem to be keeping up with the other students academically.

The principal of Rose Place was hired recently and is the first minority administrator in the school district. Previously, he had a successful career as an administrator in inner-city schools, and he had a reputation for working well with the school superintendents. The principal was referred to the school board by the mayor of the city, who knew the principal. The mayor mentioned to the president of the school board that it would be politically advantageous if Rose Place hired a principal that the mayor recommended.

The staff at Smith-Jackson Elementary School is 100% Caucasian, which presents another problem for the students who use the voluntary busing program. A few of the students have expressed their opinion to the principal that they wished more of the teachers had the same background as they do.

For this case, assume that you are the newly hired principal and that your ethnicity matches that of many of the students who are in the voluntary busing program.

The Problem

A number of children who ride the bus and participate in the voluntary busing program have academic and disciplinary problems at school. Some of the teachers have expressed to you how pleased they are to have someone of your ethnicity at the school so that you can relate to the newcomers. Parents of students who are bused see you as an advocate not only for their children, but also for themselves.

During one of the school meetings community members were invited to attend, a parent raised the issue of losing funding for the next school year because of a decline in the projected number of students who planned to attend Smith-Jackson. She reported that a recent parent survey indicated that 75% of the students currently enrolled in the voluntary busing program did not plan to attend Smith-Jackson the following school year.

One of the parents, who had lived in Rose Place for many years and was the son of the former white supremacy group's president, responded to the issue by stating that he thought the school was better off without the voluntary busing program. He added that many of the students that came to Smith-Jackson from outside of the community caused trouble at school and did not do well academically. He also said that he thought things were much better before the government stepped in and tried to change Rose Place by integrating Smith-Jackson.

Several days later, you met this same parent outside the classroom where he served as a parent volunteer. After you greeted him, he stated, "I don't have to talk to you, you know. This is a free country, and I wish you and your kind would just go back where you came from. Why don't you leave and take the students who look like you with you."

Case Analysis Framework
1. Summarize the case.
2. Identify the problem in a single sentence.
3. Select specific information from the case and categorize it according to people, place, or program.
4. Review and prioritize the information.
5. Refer to the data in each category to solve the problem identified in the case and to respond to the case study questions.

Questions to Research and Consider
1. What is your initial reaction to the parent?
2. What insights do you gain from this experience about some of the community's opinions about the voluntary busing program?
3. What are your role and responsibility to the students in the community? To the students who are bused?
4. How do you go about gathering information on the feelings and experiences of the students who are bused?
5. How do you monitor race and human relations at your school?
6. Should you inform the superintendent of your encounter with the parent?
7. Does the parent have a legitimate concern?

8. How will you address his concern regarding the students who are bused to Smith-Jackson?
9. Should you plan a race relations development day for your staff?
10. What is your district's policy on hate crimes?

Developing Your Leadership Expertise: ISLLC Standards 1, 2, & 4

Develop a plan for creating a forum to address race relations in your community. Identify priorities, list goals and objectives, and include the primary purpose for wanting to improve race relations in your community.

MAY THE BEST CLERK WIN

George Washington Elementary School is located in the center of a large metropolitan city. Many of its students are from immigrant families who have recently moved to the area.

Because of the massive influx of students, the school has been struggling with increased enrollment. Currently the students number 1,300, but the school was constructed to hold only 700 students. As a consequence, nine portable classrooms have been added to the existing school site.

To make matters worse, the school district has implemented a class-size reduction program. Because of the facilities issues at George Washington, the school district developed a plan to relocate the nine portable classrooms to the junior high school site. As part of the plan, the fourth and fifth graders will be transferred, leaving more room at George Washington to accommodate the class-size reduction program.

This proposal was met with some resistance from a few of the parents, who were not pleased that their elementary grade–level children would be attending the junior high school. However, the school district felt that this was the only solution to the enrollment problem.

As part of the plan and in support of the students who were being moved to the junior high school site, the district also transferred nine classroom teachers and one school clerk to the junior high.

Assume for this case that you are the principal of the junior high school.

The Problem

Rosa Hernandez has been a school clerk at George Washington Elementary School for the past 10 years. She has a great deal of influence with the staff and the teachers at the school. She speaks Spanish fluently and is often called on by school administrators and teachers to translate for the Spanish-speaking parents and their children.

Rosa was one of the school clerks selected to move to the junior high. Stella Lopez was hired to replace Rosa. Stella arrived at the elementary school two weeks prior to Rosa's leaving. Rosa resented Stella as soon as she arrived at the school and began spreading rumors about her. This was brought to the principal's attention by one of the teachers, but when Rosa was confronted with the matter, she denied spreading rumors and said, in fact, that she felt picked on by Stella. She also accused Stella of not showing her the respect she deserved.

Two weeks later, the junior high school site was ready for the newcomers. As soon as Rosa relocated to her new office, she began calling the elementary school to complain about her new office. She said that she never should have been moved to the junior high school and that she was not satisfied with her new assignment. She added that she heard that Stella was not doing a good job and that many of the parents were not happy with her.

A few weeks later, the district sent to each of its school sites federal survey cards that were to be sent home with the students, signed by the parents, and returned to the schools. It was the school clerk's responsibility to collect the cards from the students and to contact the parents by phone if they failed to return the cards to the school. Rosa was assigned this task at the junior high school.

Rosa had dealt with this process numerous times before, and she felt that she was an expert. For Stella, however, this was a new assignment. Rosa was determined to collect all of the federal survey cards at her school before Stella collected the cards at her site.

Within a short period of time, Rosa reported that all the survey cards had been signed by the parents of students at the junior high school and returned to the school. She bragged about being the first clerk in the district to have completed the task. Rosa, of course, mentioned that Stella had not received all of the survey cards back from the parents at the elementary school.

Two days later, a parent of one of the junior high school students met with the principal. After the meeting ended, she handed a survey card to the principal. She apologized to the principal for returning the card at such a late date and explained that she had been away on vacation and had just returned.

The principal decided to file the card with the other survey cards because Rosa was at lunch and not at her desk. When the principal opened the box where the completed survey cards were filed, she discovered that a survey card had already been filed under the parent's name. She compared the signature on the card in the box with the one that was just handed to her by the parent, and it was obvious that the signatures were not the same. After taking a close look at all of the survey cards, the principal located 25 cards that she believed had been signed by Rosa.

Case Analysis Framework

1. Summarize the case.
2. Identify the problem in a single sentence.
3. Select specific information from the case and categorize it according to people, place, or program.
4. Review and prioritize the information.
5. Refer to the data in each category to solve the problem identified in the case and to respond to the case study questions.

Questions to Research and Consider

1. What do you do with this information?
2. Will you contact Rosa's former supervisor regarding the incident?
3. What ethical issues are involved?
4. What are the legal ramifications for forging the signature of a parent?
5. Do you think the staff will support Rosa?
6. What, if anything, do you tell your superintendent about the situation?
7. Are there grounds for suspending or firing Rosa if she forged signatures?
8. How has Rosa's behavior influenced your efforts to unite the staff?
9. What can you do to improve the relationship between Rosa and Stella?
10. What can be done to ensure that the two school sites are functioning as one?

Developing Your Leadership Expertise:
ISLLC Standards 1 & 6

Describe how you would document this situation and present your findings to the superintendent.

No Matter What, It Isn't Working

The community of Castletown is extremely supportive of its high school, Montclair High. Many parents in the community attended Montclair in their youth and remain involved in school activities, especially those related to athletics. Parental input is ongoing and influential. Community members do not hesitate to contact school board members about various issues, including some that may be considered irrelevant. The composition of the student population at the high school has remained stable for the past five years. Although the teaching staff is primarily Caucasian, many of the teachers speak Spanish fluently.

Montclair High School is the only comprehensive high school in a 175-square-mile region. It serves a large, semirural, unincorporated area. It has an enrollment of 1,900 students with a teaching staff of 90, including 6 special education teachers. There are 3 assistant principals, 3 counselors, a part-time athletic director, and a fairly large clerical staff. The school district is facing a bond election this year. The administration needs the support of the community in order to pass this bond. Many classified employees work in this district, and the school district needs the vote of every citizen. Serious problems exist with the classified staff at the site, and the previous administrator resigned because of unresolved issues dealing with the evaluations of classified employees who had been at the high school for a long time.

For the following situation, assume you are a first-year principal at Montclair High School.

The Problem

For this school year the district hired a new school counselor, Steve Morris, to fill a vacated position at Montclair High School. The previous counselor retired after serving the high school for almost 30 years. Steve was hired one week before school started and had little or no training for the job. His primary responsibility was to help students with their academic schedules.

Steve's outgoing personality, positive attitude, and hands-on approach was in direct contrast to the previous counselor's style. During Steve's first week in the position, Martha, a member of the classified counseling staff, commented on Steve's approach to students and alluded to his familiarity with them. This included placing his hands on their shoulders or patting them on the back. She became increasingly agitated when she saw him hug a student in his office. During lunch she would share her observations with the other female classified staff in the office. Soon, all the classified staff were making comments concerning Steve's behavior.

Steve's lack of experience in academic counseling and his unfamiliarity with the computer software system caused him to make several serious mistakes in student scheduling. Martha chastised him in front of students for his errors. Following one of these episodes, Steve approached Martha, placed his hands on her shoulders, and instructed her to calm down. She immediately contacted you to express her displeasure with Steve's actions. She also commented that Steve was making serious mistakes in student scheduling and in his record keeping.

As the principal, you are extremely cautious in dealing with Martha because you are aware of her history of problems with the former principal. Two years ago, the previous administrator gave Martha a poor evaluation. He removed her from the counseling staff and placed her in the library. Martha took her complaint to the classified union, which resulted in a series of meetings with district-level administrators.

To further complicate the issue, Martha is claiming that several female students personally have told her they do not like Mr. Morris touching them. She also claims that parents are calling the other school counselors to complain about Steve's scheduling mistakes. You decide to conduct numerous interviews with classified staff, who confirm what Martha has shared with you.

Case Analysis Framework

1. Summarize the case.
2. Identify the problem in a single sentence.
3. Select specific information from the case and categorize it according to people, place, or program.
4. Review and prioritize the information.
5. Refer to the data in each category to solve the problem identified in the case and to respond to the case study questions.

Questions to Research and Consider

1. What do you do now?
2. What are your legal and ethical considerations?
3. Do you have in-service policies and practices for new employees?
4. Is it a good idea to require written statements from the people involved?
5. What is your opinion of Martha's actions? Mr. Morris' actions?
6. What concerns do you have regarding employees who have a strong voice in school matters?
7. Should you inform the superintendent of these concerns?
8. How do you proceed if you discover that Martha is not telling the truth?
9. How do you proceed if you discover Martha is telling the truth?
10. How might this affect the bond election?

Developing Your Leadership Expertise:
ISLLC Standards 3 & 5

Research the Supreme Court's ruling addressing a school district's responsibility regarding sexual harassment in the workplace.

THE PARENT WHO RAN AWAY WITH THE CHILD

In the Stanton Unified School District, parents play an important role in the intellectual, social, and personal growth of their children. Workshops and classes are provided by each school in the district to help parents develop skills so that they can assist their children with school-related objectives. Additionally, parents are encouraged to participate in a wide variety of school activities.

Kanner Elementary School is considered by the parents of Kanner's students to be the best elementary school in the district. Sixty-five percent of the students come from a variety of ethnic backgrounds and the remaining 35% are Caucasian. The school is proud of its rich diversity, and many families have lived in the community all their lives.

Approximately 95% of Kanner's kindergarten through fifth-grade students are eligible to receive free or reduced-cost meals. The school is situated in a low-income urban neighborhood and is approximately 60 years old.

For this case, assume you are the principal of Kanner Elementary School.

The Problem

You began your assignment as the principal of Kanner Elementary School two years ago, and you are a first-time administrator. The previous principal was on the site for 22 years and was well respected by staff and parents. As a new administrator, you are striving to implement a newly revised educational plan and you take pride in working in harmony with parents to achieve this goal.

Recently, a new second-grade student named Tyson enrolled at Kanner Elementary School. Tyson transferred from a nearby private school, and it was immediately apparent to Tyson's teacher that he was experiencing problems adjusting to his new classroom. After just one week at school, Tyson's teacher informed you that Tyson was having difficulty sitting still, concentrating in class, and following directions. Tyson's teacher was visibly upset and asked you for suggestions on how to handle Tyson.

You decide to contact the principal at Tyson's former school and speak with her about Tyson's behavior to determine if he has had previous problems in school. She hesitates to respond to your questions at first but then offers the following information:

1. Tyson had been referred to the school psychologist for his uncontrollable classroom behavior, but his parents removed him from the school before the psychologist could assess Tyson.
2. Tyson's former principal had been informed by Tyson's parents that a neurologist had seen Tyson and diagnosed him as having Attention Deficit Hyperactivity Disorder (ADHD). The psychologist also had recommended that Tyson be placed on medication.
3. Tyson's former teacher had placed Tyson on a behavior modification plan, but his behavior had not improved.

Following the conversation with Tyson's former school principal, you contact Tyson's parents to arrange a conference with them and Tyson's teacher. You are able to speak only with Tyson's father, and he offers the following information regarding Tyson:

1. Tyson was not successful at his previous school because Tyson's teacher had not shown his parents any respect.
2. Tyson will not be given any medication no matter who recommends it.
3. Tyson is behind in reading and math because he was often sent to the "fun center" at his previous school instead of being forced to remain in class and work.
4. Tyson's father informs you that he had problems when he was a child in school and that he was placed in special classes, none of which he felt had done him any good.
5. He stated that he would speak with his wife about coming to the school for a conference. He also informed you that she would agree

with him that if Tyson were having problems at Kanner Elementary School then it would be better for Tyson if he were transferred to another school in the district.

Case Analysis Framework

1. Summarize the case.
2. Identify the problem in a single sentence.
3. Select specific information from the case and categorize it according to people, place, or program.
4. Review and prioritize the information.
5. Refer to the data in each category to solve the problem identified in the case and to respond to the case study questions.

Questions to Research and Consider

1. How will you respond to Tyson's teacher?
2. What immediate intervention should be used by Tyson's teacher to address his problems in the classroom?
3. Is it appropriate for the neurologist to recommend medication for Tyson?
4. What can you do to develop the trust of Tyson's parents?
5. What additional information should be elicited from Tyson's parents?
6. What should happen immediately to help Tyson succeed in school?
7. Should you contact the school psychologist at Tyson's former school and speak with her about Tyson's behavior?
8. Would Tyson qualify for assistance under Section 504 of the Rehabilitation Act of 1973?
9. What, if any, ethical issues are presented in this case?
10. What information will you share with the school administrator at Tyson's next school if his parents choose to transfer him to another school?

Developing Your Leadership Expertise: ISLLC Standards 4 & 6

> Organize a parent in-service program that addresses how to deal effectively with children like Tyson.

AN EDUCATIONAL LEADER'S LEGACY

Nowhere in the country where school leaders meet and convene is there a place that comes close to the Raymond Hill Institute. Every year 100 educators from throughout the country are chosen to collectively debate, discuss, and engage in studying the most important issues facing our institutions of teaching and learning.

The Raymond Hill Institute is located just east of one of the most prominent communities in America. It is rich in cultural diversity, devoid of stagnant ideals, and founded in the rarest fashion of transformation and change. The Raymond Hill Institute, formed in memory of the visionary Ethel Pearl, was born from an idea conceived by a school principal whose last wish was that there be a place to meet with her colleagues from various communities in the country to exchange ideas, develop new visions, and create new ways of thinking in order to advance the science and art of learning in the area of educational leadership.

The Problem

Ethel Pearl had been a teacher most of her adult life. She began her career teaching in a one-room schoolhouse in Nebraska. When she married, she migrated to the East and found herself in an inner-city school challenged by a community that seemed to have lost its fight for the pursuit of learning and to have exchanged it for surviving the pursuit of life in the streets. During her tenure as a teacher, Ethel witnessed in her students disappointment, anger, withdrawal, and, eventually, complete defeat.

A few years into teaching, Ethel became more discouraged with what she saw and decided to make a change that she hoped would influence the lives of the students around her. On the day she decided to begin her mission, she was determined to start each school day with simple acts of kindness.

If a student came to school hungry, Ethel would bring food and make certain that the child ate. She discovered early on that not all children take advantage of the breakfast program offered to economically disadvantaged students. She learned that just because food is offered, many students do not feel as though adults care whether or not they eat. And so Ethel would show that she cared, and the students would eat.

If students were indifferent to learning, Ethel would find a way to motivate them. If this meant buying token gifts for the students to boost morale, she would do it. And if students failed to come to school, she would visit their homes to find out why the students were not attending school and develop a plan to change the problem.

Ethel didn't begin her mission with every student in the school; she began with one student, then two, and then three. After a while, the students came to school because they wanted to. She would fill the voids for what students didn't have. Her students would remember many years later that the most important gift she gave was the gift of hope. And many of them who would later become teachers themselves promised to pass this lesson on to their students.

When Ethel Pearl was asked to take a lead teacher position at a new school, she took many of her colleagues with her. They followed her because they saw something in her that made them want to be around her. Her love for learning and her acts of kindness were contagious.

It wasn't many years later when Ethel Pearl was approached by the superintendent to become a school principal. She had no desire to leave teaching, but common sense told her that becoming a school leader would give her yet another opportunity to teach, although in a different way than the one she was used to.

Ethel Pearl continued to use her acts of kindness with her staff. When a teacher came to school unable to teach because she had lost her interest in teaching, Ethel would find a way to motivate her. In some cases, she asked her teachers to identify what it was that they loved to do just as she had asked her students what they had loved to do. Her method was to find that "something" and use that love to ignite learning. If she found out that an unmotivated teacher loved art, she would locate a conference on art and send the teacher to the conference. Upon returning from the conference, Ethel would ask the teacher to share her love of art with other teachers. Thus, a teacher became newly born. As a consequence the love for teaching and learning was returned to the classroom.

It was during her last year as a school administrator that a group of former students and colleagues came together and founded the Raymond Hill Institute in honor of Ethel Pearl. As a tribute to Ethel's leadership and as a reminder to others for what she stood for, the following Attributes of an Effective Leader are posted above the door to the Raymond Hill Institute:

Attributes of an Effective Leader

1. Practice daily acts of kindness.
2. Consider each and every day a teaching opportunity.
3. Make it your mission to mentor and seek out apprentices.
4. Engage life and make common sense and decency your mantras.
5. Celebrate debate, dialogue, and great discussions surrounding the science of teaching and learning.
6. See every student as one who will teach throughout his or her lifetime.
7. Applaud the opportunity to be lead, and humbly step up and lead when your vision will improve the lives of others.

The Raymond Hill Institute still exists today and is funded by private donations offered over the years by friends, family, and followers of Ethel Pearl. Her leadership legacy speaks for itself.

You might wonder about the origin of the name of the Institute. Raymond Hill was the name of the place where Ethel Pearl first taught in the one-room schoolhouse in Nebraska.

Assume for this case you are an aspiring school administrator.

Case Analysis Framework
1. Summarize the case.
2. Identify the problem in a single sentence.

3. Select specific information from the case and categorize it according to people, place, or program.
4. Review and prioritize the information.
5. Refer to the data in each category to solve the problem identified in the case and to respond to the case study questions.

Questions to Research and Consider

1. Have you known an educator like Ethel Pearl? What influence did he or she have on you as an educator?
2. Do you meet with other educators to discuss educational issues and trends?
3. What attributes did Ethel Pearl demonstrate that you believe create effective educational administrators?
4. What other qualities do you believe are essential for effective leadership?
5. Identify a mentor and share with your colleagues the influence that person had on your career as an educator.
6. Do you believe there is a relationship between effective teaching and effective educational leadership? Why, why not?
7. What are the advantages of developing a list of leadership qualities?
8. How do you mentor other educators? What impact does your mentoring have within your school and school district?
9. Do you support the idea that educators will benefit by meeting together for the purpose of debating and discussing education? Why or why not?
10. Identify from the list posted above the door at Raymond Hill Institute one of the attributes pertaining to educational leadership that you believe is the most important and support your selection.

Developing Your Leadership Expertise: ISLLC Standard 1

Develop a list of attributes that you believe are critical to effective educational leadership. Identify how you would put the attribute into practice.

WHEN STUDENTS TAKE MATTERS INTO THEIR OWN HANDS

Rockbed is a suburban community in southern California. It consists of residential housing, including single-family dwellings, apartments, and condominiums. There is virtually no industry in the area. The businesses in the community include supermarkets, restaurants, fast-food establishments, and other service-type shops.

Dry Creek Middle School is located in the center of the community and educates students that are enrolled in seventh and eighth grade. The staff at the school consists of 14 regular education teachers, 1 principal, 1 vice principal, 1 special education teacher, and 1 part-time psychologist. The clerical staff includes 2 administrative assistants, a health clerk, a media clerk, and a custodial staff of two.

The school was built five years ago, and the staff has developed a close relationship over the years. Because of the small number of students enrolled at Dry Creek, scheduling is a challenge, but the staff has worked in harmony to meet this challenge in order to provide a quality program for its students.

The faculty who teach at Dry Creek are dedicated. Mr. Lincoln and Mrs. Washington teach eighth-grade language arts and history, respectively. Mr. Molecule teaches eighth-grade science and Ms. Digits, who is the most popular teacher at Dry Creek, teaches math. Mrs. Grammar and Mr. Caesar teach seventh-grade language arts and social studies classes, and Mr. Einstein teaches seventh-grade math.

The students assigned to special education classes meet with Mr. Sped during the first four periods of each day and are enrolled in elective classes for the last two periods of the school day. The regular education teachers work well with Mr. Sped in sharing the responsibility of offering quality programs and services to the special education students.

During the current school year the numbers of students enrolled in the seventh and eighth grade are considerably different. There are only 110 students enrolled in the seventh grade, whereas there are 160 students enrolled in the eighth grade. The difference in the number of students presents a challenge for the principal at Dry Creek, who worked hard with the staff to prepare a schedule that would be supported by all the teachers.

At the beginning of the school year the principal asked a few of the seventh-grade teachers to teach the eighth grade, and because of the team spirit and cooperative working environment at Dry Creek, the teachers agreed to make the change for the sake of the students. This was typical of Dry Creek teachers.

For this case, assume that you are the principal at Dry Creek Middle School.

The Problem

By the middle of the school year, another middle school in the school district, Baxter Middle School, experienced significant growth because of the completion of a new housing development in the community.

The superintendent was receiving pressure from the parents of the students enrolled at Baxter Middle School to reduce the number of students in each class and to increase the number of teachers in the school. The superintendent decided to transfer one of the teachers from Dry Creek Middle School to Baxter in response to the pressure from the parents of Baxter's students.

When transfers of teachers are necessary, the district policy states that the teacher(s) who will be transferred are the ones with the least seniority. Ms. Digits had the least seniority at Dry Creek, and therefore the superintendent chose to transfer Ms. Digits to Baxter.

The solution to Baxter's enrollment problem was good for Baxter but not good for Dry Creek. When the teachers at Dry Creek discovered the superintendent's plan to transfer Ms. Digits, they met with you, the principal, to make known their objections. You explained to the teachers that you already voiced your concern to the superintendent, but she informed you that her mind was made up and that she was following the district's transfer policy.

The teachers were not satisfied with your response to their concern, and they selected a few representatives to meet with the superintendent, over your objection.

At the meeting with the superintendent, the teachers informed the superintendent that Ms. Digits was a valued faculty member at Dry Creek, and they implored her not to transfer Ms. Digits. The superintendent ignored their pleas, directed them to leave her office, and ordered them back to Dry Creek.

The teachers returned to their school and begin to share with the students the fact that Ms. Digits would be transferred to Baxter. When the students discovered the superintendent's plan to transfer one of their favorite teachers, they decided to take matters into their own hands.

At approximately 8:00 a.m on a Monday morning you receive a phone call from the superintendent, who informs you that there are at least 60 students marching in front of the district office, along with about 30 parents who have joined the students to protest Ms. Digit's transfer. She instructs you to report to the district office as soon as possible to remediate the situation. She adds that if the students and the parents are not dispersed from the district office by 9:30 a.m, you can look for a new job.

You immediately leave your office. You stop by Mr. Sped's classroom to invite him to accompany you to help with the dispersion of the students and parents at the district office. You discover that Mr. Sped is not in his classroom. Instead, his instructional aide is sitting at his desk, and she informs you that she is planning on teaching Mr. Sped's class because Mr. Sped is leading the demonstration at the district office.

Case Analysis Framework

1. Summarize the case.
2. Identify the problem in a single sentence.
3. Select specific information from the case and categorize it according to people, place, or program.
4. Review and prioritize the information.
5. Refer to the data in each category to solve the problem identified in the case and to respond to the case study questions.

Questions to Research and Consider

1. How do you handle the situation at this point?
2. What is your opinion of the manner in which the superintendent dealt with the teachers who met with her to express their concern about Ms. Digit's transfer?
3. What factors in this case made it difficult for the teachers to accept the superintendent's decision?
4. What steps will you take to defuse the volatile situation?
5. What responsibility does the school have for the behavior of its students when they are off school grounds?
6. How do you deal with the parents who are involved in the protest?
7. The school day does not start until 8:30 a.m; what can you do to keep other students from going to the district office and joining the protest?
8. What consequences should the students who are participating in the protest face?
9. Are you and the district office liable for any injury that might occur to the students who are participating in the demonstration?
10. What actions will you take in addressing the issue of the teacher who led the protest?

Developing Your Leadership Expertise: ISLLC Standards 1, 2, 3, & 6

Prepare a report for the superintendent. Explain how you dispersed the students at the district office and brought them back to school.

IN THE WRONG PLACE AT THE WRONG TIME

The community of Mountain View has a population of 90,000. It is a relatively young community as compared with the rest of the county. People move to Mountain View to get away from the hustle and bustle of the city.

Mountain View High School was five years old when it began to operate as a 9th- through 12th-grade school. With a current enrollment of 2,740 students, the school is located on 92.5 acres of land and accommodates a $40 million facility containing 61 classrooms, 26 labs, and 6 classrooms specifically designed for special education students.

The school has a diverse population of 40% Caucasian, 30% Hispanic, 27% African American, and 3% Native American students. During its first year of operation, the school experienced some racial tension. However, the school culture has evolved to a point where this tension has waned. Mountain View's staff includes 111 teachers, 5 administrators, 5 counselors, 1 librarian, 1 school psychologist, and 48 classified employees.

In addition to a strong core curriculum, Mountain View offers a wide variety of college preparatory classes. All extracurricular sports are offered onsite, except the aquatic programs, which are scheduled at a nearby community pool. Mountain View's athletic program, band, choir, and academic teams are all highly competitive and are recognized at the local, state, and national levels for their outstanding performances.

For the following case assume you are the principal at Mountain View High School.

The Problem

Bart Smith is an 18-year-old senior with a history of mistreating women. There have been several occasions in which Bart has demonstrated inappropriate behavior, particularly toward a female student named Lupe. Lupe has been described by her teachers as quiet and respectful.

Bart transferred recently from another school within the district because his family was not satisfied with the way Bart had been treated at the first school. His parents insisted that Bart was the victim of racial prejudice at his former school.

On a Tuesday morning, the assistant principal received a call from a staff member who reported seeing a male student entering the ladies' restroom.

A female campus supervisor was sent to the restroom to investigate the matter. After searching the restroom, the campus supervisor reported that she was unable to locate a male student there. Later that same period, another call was received in the principal's office from a different teacher who reported seeing a male student leaving the ladies' restroom. This time, the student was identified as Bart.

By the end of lunch period, a rumor was spreading across the campus that Bart was seen in the ladies' restroom with Lupe and that they were involved in a fight. Bart was seen hitting Lupe and knocking her to the ground.

As a result of the rumor and after having received the two calls reporting that Bart was in the ladies' restroom, you decided to send for Bart and Lupe.

Within a few minutes, both of the students arrived at your office and waited for you to meet with them. In the meantime, the parents of both students had been contacted, and they also were waiting to meet with you.

While all of this was taking place, one of Lupe's girlfriends was in the counseling office informing one of the school counselors that Lupe told her that she had been beaten by Bart on many occasions. In fact, according to Lupe's friend, Bart had broken Lupe's hand, and Lupe had told her parents that she had fallen down at school. Lupe's friend informed the counselor that Bart had threatened Lupe's life and that she was afraid for Lupe.

The school counselor shared this conversation with you just before you were to meet with Bart, Lupe, and their parents.

Case Analysis Framework

1. Summarize the case.
2. Identify the problem in a single sentence.
3. Select specific information from the case and categorize it according to people, place, or program.
4. Review and prioritize the information.
5. Refer to the data in each category to solve the problem identified in the case and to respond to the case study questions.

Questions to Research and Consider

1. How would you approach the supervisor who failed to find Bart and Lupe in the ladies' restroom?
2. Was there adequate supervision to prevent this incident from occurring?
3. How would you respond to the school counselor after she informed you of the conversation between herself and Lupe's friend?
4. What information should be released to the staff concerning this incident?
5. Who should be notified regarding this incident besides the parents of the students involved?
6. What problems do you anticipate from the parents?
7. At what point do you notify the district office?
8. How do you respond to the media if they contact you?
9. Would you prepare a memo for the personnel file? Why or why not?
10. Should there be any counseling service provided to the students? If so, what kind?

Developing Your Leadership Expertise: ISLLC Standards 1, 3, & 5

Determine how you would respond if a television reporter and a camera crew came onto the campus at the end of the school day and started interviewing students regarding the incident.

THE BEST OF FRIENDS
AT THE WORST OF TIMES

The city of San Miguel is located 18 miles east of the county courthouse. It has a population just shy of 50,000 residents. The streets are lined with trees, and ample housing is available for the friendly, family-oriented people in the immediate area.

The socioeconomic climate of San Miguel is upper middle class, and the San Miguel School District reflects the appearance and values of the community. The first school in the district opened in 1891 with 1 teacher and 14 students. Today the district consists of 11 schools educating students in kindergarten through grade 8. There have been several attempts to organize the district into kindergarten through fifth-grade schools and to create a middle school for grades 6 to 8. However, these proposals have not received the support of the community. Most of the parents believe that their children are safe and secure in the existing kindergarten through eighth-grade schools, and they do not endorse the idea of change.

The parents have high expectations for their children. All the schools in the district have received State Distinguished School Recognition Awards, and five of the schools have received National School Achievement Awards. The test scores have consistently been high throughout the district, and the district ranks in the top 10% of the county's school districts in terms of its test scores.

Cold Creek School is one of the 11 schools in the district. It enjoys a stellar reputation. There are no apartment buildings or multifamily dwellings within its attendance boundaries. A two-parent family with a stay-at-home mom is the norm for students at Cold Creek, and it is not uncommon for the school to enroll children whose parents also attended the school. A few of the other schools within the district view Cold Creek as somewhat elitist, and the staff has experienced increased pressure from its students to maintain its standing as number one in the district.

Each year the district publishes state test results by school and by teacher. Although the test scores remain high at Cold Creek, maintaining this level of achievement year after year has created a great deal of pressure for the teachers and administration at the school. The parents have access to the test scores by class, and they use this information to request particular teachers for their children at the school.

For this case, assume that you are the principal of Cold Creek School. At your school, there are 1 vice principal and 48 teachers on staff. You are well liked by the teachers and accepted by the community, and you feel your position is safe as long as the test scores at your school remain among the highest in the district; in fact, the superintendent has just informed you that your school ranks number one in this respect.

The Problem

Mrs. Burton is the most requested teacher for second grade at your school. She is respected, enthusiastic, energetic, and child centered. Her classroom is well organized, and she uses a variety of effective teaching techniques to meet the needs of all her students. When test scores are published, Mrs. Burton's scores are always at the top. She is very proud of this fact and has shared with you that she hopes her performance will help her to move into an administrative position some day.

You have developed a strong friendship with Mrs. Burton during the 10 years that you have been at Cold Creek. It is not unusual for your family and hers to spend weekend days together riding bikes, picnicking, and sharing family celebrations.

Mrs. Burton shares an academic building with three other teachers. Temporary walls separate the classrooms, and the second-grade teachers work in teams from time to time. Only one of the teachers gets along well with Mrs. Burton. The other two teachers view her as somewhat of a prima donna.

Toward the end of each school year, you devote a tremendous amount of time and effort into organizing the state testing schedule for students at Cold

Creek School. You develop clear, written procedures that you distribute to all staff members at mandatory staff meetings. At each meeting you review the testing procedures and schedule with all the teachers. Parent volunteers and classified employees are selected to help proctor the testing for each classroom. The proctors are responsible for picking up the test materials, supervising the testing, and delivering the test materials back to the testing center at the end of each day.

This year you decide to implement a process that will increase test security, following the lead of some of the other principals in the district who have developed new test-security procedures. You develop a procedure that addresses the transporting of test materials from the testing center to the classrooms. The process requires that you personally place your initials next to the name of the classroom teacher whom the proctor represents when the test materials are picked up by the proctors. You follow this same procedure when the proctors return the test materials to the testing center at the end of each day.

This year, the testing schedule was planned for an eight-day period. On Thursday of the second week of testing, about an hour after the students were dismissed from school, you entered Mrs. Burton's classroom just to visit. You noticed that Mrs. Burton was at her desk with a pencil in hand and a student's open test booklet in front of her. Mrs. Burton immediately jumped to her feet and used her body to block your view of her desk and the student booklets. She appeared nervous and obviously felt uncomfortable that you were in her classroom.

You immediately inquired as to why she was looking through the test booklet. She informed you that she was simply checking some of her students' answers because the students seemed to erase a lot, and she wanted to make certain that the answers appeared on the tests. She also said that the proctor, a parent and PTA officer, had left the test booklets on a chair at the end of the morning testing period. She added that she was just looking through the booklets of her best-performing students because of her concern that they finished early.

You remind Mrs. Burton that test security is very important, and you return the test booklets to the testing center. After you return to your office, you request a meeting with the vice principal to tell her about Mrs. Burton and the test booklet incident. The two of you conclude that the test security procedure had been violated and that you should investigate the matter further.

Case Analysis Framework

1. Summarize the case.
2. Identify the problem in a single sentence.
3. Select specific information from the case and categorize it according to people, place, or program.
4. Review and prioritize the information.
5. Refer to the data in each category to solve the problem identified in the case and to respond to the case study questions.

Questions to Research and Consider

1. To investigate the situation further, you plan to speak with Mrs. Burton. When will you do this and what will you tell her?
2. How does your personal relationship with Mrs. Burton affect your decision to investigate her behavior?
3. Who else, if anyone, will you need to interview regarding the violation of the test-security procedures?
4. When you meet with Mrs. Burton, she denies any wrongdoing. What do you do now?
5. Will you notify anyone at the district office that you suspect Mrs. Burton cheated?
6. What do you tell the proctor for Mrs. Burton's class, if anything?
7. What is your position regarding parent requests for teachers whose students have high test scores?
8. What do you tell the other teachers at your school about Mrs. Burton?
9. How will Mrs. Burton's behavior affect your relationship with her?
10. What could you have done to prevent this from happening at your school?

Developing Your Leadership Expertise:
ISLLC Standards 1, 4, & 5

Investigate your district's policy regarding testing procedures. Determine if each school in your district follows the same procedures.

FROM ROOKIE TO REALITY

Shoreline Elementary is a small school, with 720 students, serving kindergarten through fifth grade. Comparatively speaking, it has a much smaller student population than the other 18 schools in the district.

Shoreline opened in 1970 and has maintained a reputation as one of the most desirable schools in the area. There have been only a few reported incidences of behavioral problems, and parents are actively involved in the parent volunteer program. They take an active role in their children's education and are generally supportive of the school's various educational programs.

You were hired as an assistant principal at another school in the district, but because of the illness of Shoreline's principal, you have been asked to assume the role of interim principal at Shoreline for the remainder of the school year. The district does not believe that the former principal will return to work.

The transition for you has been relatively smooth. You simply had to accept and adjust to the additional responsibilities of the job. Your confidence, in part, comes from the training you received from Rick King, who is the principal at the school of your previous employment. He spent a great deal of time with you and shared the knowledge and skills he learned from watching other successful administrators in the district.

You are confident that the title *interim* will be removed if you meet or exceed the superintendent's expectations. You concentrate on being highly visible, and your hands-on approach to problem solving is received well by the staff and the community. You visit each classroom on a daily basis, carry a walkie-talkie, welcome students every morning, and respond quickly to the concerns of the parents and staff.

The Problem

After you had been at Shoreline for only two weeks, you heard that Rick King had to evacuate the students because a pipe bomb had been placed outside one of the classrooms. The bomb squad had to be summoned, and what turned out to be a homemade bomb was defused. Fortunately, no one was hurt.

This incident was covered extensively by the radio and television stations and the local newspapers. The concern that this type of event might recur in the district was at the forefront of every administrator's mind.

Shortly after the incident at Rick's school and 20 minutes before the beginning of school at your site, you walked out in front of the school to welcome the students and parents. You noticed a fourth-grade student running toward you with an adult whom you believed to be his mother. The two shouted in your direction and pointed at an object that was lying on the sidewalk just across the street. After you calmed the child and the parent down, you walked across the street in an effort to get a better look at the object.

You walked quickly to where the object was located and noticed that it was near the crosswalk and appeared to be made of metal. Each end was wrapped with tape. You immediately assumed that it was another homemade explosive device similar to the one at Rick's school.

Case Analysis Framework

1. Summarize the case.
2. Identify the problem in a single sentence.
3. Select specific information from the case and categorize it according to people, place, or program.
4. Review and prioritize the information.
5. Refer to the data in each category to solve the problem identified in the case and to respond to the case study questions.

Questions to Research and Consider

1. What is the first thing you should do?
2. What criteria, if any, would you use in deciding whether or not to evacuate the school building?

3. Would you evacuate the entire school or just the buildings closest to the bomb?
4. List the steps you would take in informing the parents of what happened at your school.
5. Do you feel that school administrators should be required to receive training in bomb threat safety?
6. What type of follow-up intervention and in-service training should you provide for your staff?
7. What are the limitations and the liabilities for school administrators in a situation like this?
8. Is there any way that an administrator can reduce the amount of media coverage for an event like this?
9. What type of report would you be expected to forward to the district office regarding this incident?
10. When should a site administrator notify the superintendent regarding problems at the school site? List some examples.

Developing Your Leadership Expertise: ISLLC Standards 3, 4, & 5

Research your school district's policy on how to address bomb threats and distribute this information to your colleagues. Conduct a workshop specific to safety and preventative security measures.

TO BRIAN, IN HIS MEMORY

Riverdale is located beyond the city and just below the mountain range that surrounds the valley of Buena Vista. It is not uncommon to see children on their way home from school riding horses or piling into the back of a truck, seemingly enjoying the innocence of youth.

The population consists of some long-time residents and a few newcomers who have moved to Riverdale to escape the city. The community shares one high school, one middle school, and three elementary schools.

The Friday night football games are attended by almost everyone in town, and at these events supportive booster club members sell raffle tickets or ask for donations for needy families in the immediate area. Most of the parents are employed in modest jobs and enjoy spending their weekends with their children.

One of the highlights of the fall season is the traditional spaghetti dinner held at the middle school, which draws a large crowd and raises money to purchase uniforms for the state- and nationally recognized high school band.

Riverdale is a quiet place, secluded from the rest of the world. The people who are lucky enough to live in this community are grateful for what they have; they do not really expect much from the outside.

Assume for this case that you are the principal of the high school.

The Problem

After the football games on Friday nights, the varsity football players frequently piled into the backs of their pickup trucks and headed for the riverbed. They have been doing this for years, and no one seemed to pay much attention to the ritual. After all, the fathers of the football players had done it too, as had their fathers before them.

After one of the biggest games of the season and after scoring the winning touchdown, Brian grabbed a beer from his dad's refrigerator and jumped into his truck. It was his turn to pick up his buddies and drive them to the riverbed.

This time, however, he did not reach his destination. Instead, Brian drove much too fast and missed a curve he had successfully negotiated a hundred times before. Brian's truck flipped over and he was thrown from the vehicle.

Brian's neighbor Sue Canner, on her way home from the game, noticed Brian's truck on the side of the road. She immediately turned her car around and drove back to the high school for help. She spotted the football coach, Mr. Bailey, who was getting into his car. She told him what she had seen, and they called 911. Within 10 minutes the local paramedics arrived at the scene of the accident. They found Brian still clutching the beer in his hand. He had already stopped breathing.

Mr. Bailey contacted Brian's parents and informed them of the tragedy. The irony of this incident was that Brian's father had just sponsored a luncheon for the parents of the football players, and the keynote speaker was a representative from the group Mothers Against Drunk Driving.

Three days later you dismissed school two hours early because you had scheduled an afternoon memorial service to be held in the gymnasium for Brian. Later that evening, and in honor of Brian, the football players drove to the riverbed. With beer in hand, each player repeated these words, "To Brian, in his memory."

Case Analysis Framework

1. Summarize the case.
2. Identify the problem in a single sentence.
3. Select specific information from the case and categorize it according to people, place, or program.
4. Review and prioritize the information.
5. Refer to the data in each category to solve the problem identified in the case and to respond to the case study questions.

Questions to Research and Consider

1. What is the responsibility of the school site administrator for educating students about drinking and driving?
2. What is the responsibility of parents for educating their children about drinking and driving?
3. What could the students have done to take responsibility for their own actions?
4. Do you believe the ritual that Brian and his friends practice is common in America's high schools?
5. What can you do as a school administrator to work with teachers to increase awareness of the dangers of drinking and driving?
6. What do you believe is the most important lesson for Brian's friends? Did they learn their lesson?
7. Do you believe that Brian's friends will continue to drink and drive?
8. Do you hold Brian's parents responsible for his accident?
9. What is the role of a coach in addressing the issue of drinking and driving?
10. Do you believe it was appropriate for the principal to schedule a memorial service in the high school gymnasium during school hours?

Developing Your Leadership Expertise: ISLLC Standards 1, 4, & 5

Share the details of this case study with parents and high school students at a workshop designed to address teenage drinking and driving. Be prepared to monitor communication between the students and parents in order to create a safe, productive, and positive environment.

THE GATEKEEPER

Monet Middle School is located in the affluent community of La Solana. This is the school's seventh year of operation, and it serves students in the sixth through eighth grades. There are 1,049 students: 23% of whom attend the school through the district's Voluntary Ethnic Enrollment Program (VEEP); 22% of whom qualify for free or reduced-cost lunches; 53% of whom qualify for the Gifted and Talented Education (GATE) program; and 5% of whom have been identified as students with special needs that qualify for special education programs.

Since Monet Middle School converted from a junior high school to a middle school in 1992, all the students, including those enrolled in special education, have been grouped heterogeneously throughout the school day, with the exception of math classes. Supplemental support services are provided during and after the school day for students who are experiencing academic difficulty. The curriculum is modified for the students with special needs, and a rigorous GATE curriculum is in place.

A large portion of the GATE budget is used to fund enrichment activities such as guest speaker assemblies, field trips, and fine arts programs for all the students attending the school. Assume for this case that you are the principal of Monet. In spite of the mandate to track students, you wish to keep the student body as heterogeneously grouped as possible. Your challenge is to balance this commitment with the new schedule requiring that students be grouped homogeneously for 200 minutes each day.

The Problem

A few years ago, Monet eliminated its tracking system, which placed students in classes according to their skill level. The most advanced students were grouped together, and the students who achieved at a lower level of performance were grouped together. Tracking was eliminated because heterogeneous grouping was believed to give all students the opportunity to learn at a high level. The school district believed tracking gave the lower-achieving students, in particular, less chance to succeed.

The administrators at Monet believed in integrating students, and it seemed that the tracking system tended to segregate students. Since doing away with the tracking system, the students at Monet have performed significantly above the national average on standardized tests. When compared with other schools in the district, Monet always has had among the highest test scores in the county for reading, language arts, and math. This includes the test scores of students who are bused to Monet through the VEEP program.

When the transition from tracking to heterogeneous grouping was first implemented, the school struggled with the change because of protests from parents of local students who opposed integrating the Hispanic and African American students with their Caucasian children. It has taken years to bridge the gap between various ethnic groups of parents at the school.

At one time, the Chicano Federation and the Anti-Defamation League had been requested to work with the diversified group of parents on behalf of the school's initiative to integrate the students academically and ethnically. However, there still remains an influential group of parents whose children are enrolled in the GATE program who are convinced that their children would be better served if they were grouped strictly according to their performance level.

In spite of Monet's success with heterogeneous grouping regarding test scores, the school board for the district recently passed an ordinance requiring all schools in the district to implement a tracking system for the upcoming school year. The program mandates a 200-minute cluster for students who are academically similar. Students identified for the GATE program are to be grouped during the 200-minute period with students who are either gifted and talented themselves or who are considered the highest-achieving students in the school. Needless to say, many of the parents whose children exhibit high academic performance are pleased with the school board's new ruling.

Case Analysis Framework

1. Summarize the case.
2. Identify the problem in a single sentence.
3. Select specific information from the case and categorize it according to people, place, or program.
4. Review and prioritize the information.
5. Refer to the data in each category to solve the problem identified in the case and to respond to the case study questions.

Questions to Research and Consider

1. What additional information do you need, if any, to determine how to proceed?
2. What input could you request from the staff prior to implementing the new schedule?
3. How could you begin bringing the parents into the process?
4. If you decide to include some of the staff and a few of the parents, what criteria would you use?
5. Assume that you strongly support heterogeneous grouping. What ethical issues would you face in deciding whether or not to use the tracking system?
6. Would you include parents in the initial stages of the transition? Why or why not?
7. Whom would you rely on, if anyone, at the district office to assist you during the transition?
8. Once you have decided on a new program schedule, when and how will you introduce it to the community?
9. Because the budget for GATE students has been used in the past to benefit all the students, explain how the distribution of funds will change with the new tracking schedule.
10. What scheduling challenges will you face?

Developing Your Leadership Expertise:
ISSLC Standards 2 & 6

Draft a letter to parents in your community that introduces a new tracking schedule and present justification for the new schedule and how it will improve student performance.

A QUESTION OF BALANCE

Westhaven is a diverse community. Several individuals within the community are quite affluent and reside on million-dollar estates. However, the majority of the students attending Walnut Creek Elementary School, which is situated in the center of Westhaven, come from modest backgrounds. Many of the students are from families who receive some form of governmental assistance, including Aid for Families with Dependent Children (AFDC).

A small number of middle-class families have recently moved to the community, and they are living in newly built, single-family homes that are located in what was once a large avocado ranch. The area is known for its agribusiness, and many of the families in the community are wealthy ranchers and farmers famous for their thoroughbred horses, avocado groves, and citrus crops.

A growing number of the students attending Walnut Creek Elementary School are from migrant families, who provide the primary labor force for the local agribusiness. The ethnic breakdown of the school reflects a balanced population of Caucasians, Hispanics, African Americans, and Vietnamese. Fifty-two percent of the school's population qualifies for free or reduced-cost lunches.

The previous principal of the school served for nine years before being asked to step down because of philosophical differences between her and some members of the school board. The staff at the school includes 45 certified teachers, a lead teacher, and 19 classified personnel.

The school currently has a population of 900 students in kindergarten through grade 6. Walnut Creek Elementary School was established in 1869 as a one-room schoolhouse, which is still part of the school's physical site and is used for school board and community meetings. Most of the rest of the campus was built in 1945, and various wings and portables have been added over the years to accommodate an increase in student enrollment.

Assume that you are the newly hired principal of Walnut Creek Elementary School.

The Problem

When you first begin your assignment as the principal of Walnut Creek, you discover a tightly controlled campus. The majority of the teachers seem oppressed; they have come to rely on the autocratic leadership style of the former principal. You believe that you were hired to inspire creativity in the staff and to help them develop an interest in the students and in their own jobs. You also believe that this change is needed and that the school board hired you to fulfill the need.

You are told that the lead teacher at your campus was offered the opportunity to continue in her position but she refused as an indication of support for the former principal, whose contract she believed should have been renewed for the tenth year. You asked her to reconsider the position, but she declined, preferring instead an assignment as a fourth-grade teacher on your campus.

One week after you are hired, a group of teachers and a few parents meet with the superintendent without your knowledge and suggest that one of your fifth-grade teachers, Mr. Humble, be assigned the position of lead teacher. He has been teaching fifth grade at the school for three years, and he seems to be the teachers' choice.

When you hear about the meeting between the teachers, parents, and superintendent, you decide to offer Mr. Humble the position, and he accepts your offer.

One of the first assignments you give Mr. Humble is to assist you in reviewing the class lists and class schedule for the coming school year. On reviewing these data with him, you notice that all the students with Vietnamese surnames are grouped together at each grade level.

You share with Mr. Humble your concern that the grouping of students by surnames does not represent an ethnically balanced enrollment. Mr. Humble simply shrugs his shoulders and states that this is the way the scheduling has always been done at Walnut Creek.

On further investigation, you discover that many students are placed in certain classes because of specific parental requests for placement. Apparently, Walnut Creek allows parents to choose their child's teacher. You have no objection to this policy, but you notice that there are no requests from the parents of the Vietnamese-speaking students.

In the meantime, a few of your teachers have confided in you that they feel the Vietnamese students are not given the same opportunity to learn as the other children. You bring this issue to the attention of Mr. Humble and he tells you to ignore the few teachers who complain.

Case Analysis Framework

1. Summarize the case.
2. Identify the problem in a single sentence.
3. Select specific information from the case and categorize it according to people, place, or program.
4. Review and prioritize the information.
5. Refer to the data in each category to solve the problem identified in the case and to respond to the case study questions.

Questions to Research and Consider

1. What will you do with the information from your teachers who complained about the imbalance in the classes?
2. What additional information will you need to address their concerns?
3. What role do you believe the teachers played in recommending the lead teacher?
4. How will you create an ethnically balanced schedule that generates support from your teachers and the parents?
5. Is it important to implement a shared decision-making model on this issue? Why or why not?
6. How will you deal with the teachers that support the previous administrator's method of developing class schedules?
7. How would you react to the news that a meeting had occurred between a few parents, a group of teachers, and the superintendent?

8. What action will you take, if any, to develop a more collegial relationship between the lead teacher and yourself?
9. How do you plan to involve the Vietnamese parents at your school?
10. What steps would you take to develop relationships with the teachers at your school who support ethnically balancing the classes to include the Vietnamese students?

Developing Your Leadership Expertise: ISLLC Standards 1, 2, 5, & 6

Plan a meeting with key individuals who you believe would be the most helpful in addressing what appears to be discrimination at the school. Include topics you will discuss, plans for improving the method of assigning students, and ideas on how to include the parents of the Vietnamese students.

GOT LUNCH?

The community of Bayshore is composed primarily of white-collar professionals. It was a planned community, and the residents are predominantly upper middle class and consider Bayshore the best place to live.

The local high school, Fairfax High, has an enrollment of approximately 3,000 students. The school was built in 1992 to accommodate 2,000 students. The campus covers approximately 60 acres and is currently the only high school in the area. An additional high school is being built and should be ready for operation in 2009. When the new school opens, changes in the attendance boundary will go into effect. There is a lobbying effort in progress in response to the new boundary proposal.

The composition of the student population of Fairfax is 25% African American, 15% Asian, 10% Hispanic, and 50% Caucasian. Occasionally, there have been conflicts on the Fairfax campus. However, when students are surveyed, they report that they get along well with each other and are very positive about the school environment.

Administrative and support staff consists of one principal, three vice principals, six counselors, one attendance coordinator, and one school police officer assigned to the school. There are 150 certificated employees at Fairfax.

Assume for the case that you are the principal at Fairfax High School.

The Problem

For the past 20 years, the district has had an open-campus lunch policy. Students were allowed to leave campus during their 30-minute lunch period and return to school by fifth period. In November, the school board intends to implement a closed-campus lunch policy. The students will no longer be allowed to leave campus during the lunch period.

The closed-campus policy is not popular among the students. The principal will be responsible for enforcing a policy that the students perceive as a denial to them of their freedom to leave the campus during their lunch period. Furthermore, the thought of having to eat the food from the cafeteria is displeasurable to some of the students, who claim that the cafeteria food is unsatisfactory.

In your role as principal, you decide to organize a committee composed of class representatives, select students, parents, teachers, and anyone else who wishes to participate. This group will meet periodically for the next several months to develop a plan to implement the closed-campus policy. The committee's task is to address the following questions:

1. How does the cafeteria plan on feeding 3,000 students in 30 minutes?
2. Where will the students eat?
3. How will the school secure the campus?
4. How will custodial services be handled?
5. How will the students occupy their time following lunch?

The following information presents portions of the minutes from the meetings as they progress.

Food Services

Currently the cafeteria has four serving lines inside the building, four serving windows, and six movable carts. The cafeteria manager stated that eight additional movable carts would be needed to accommodate the students. The newly formed committee did not think that this was enough and requested additional carts. The district denied the request.

The cafeteria manager told the committee that food services was actively looking for fast-food vendors. The group created a survey that asked students for suggestions on food items they would be interested in purchasing. In the same survey, the students were asked to vote on whether or not they wanted to start school five minutes earlier in the day and add an additional five minutes to their lunch period.

Students on the committee expressed a concern that food-service workers needed to be trained. The cafeteria manager suggested hiring student helpers. The students on the committee did not like this idea because they believed that students would not want to work during their lunchtime.

Facilities

The school is fortunate to have a cafeteria where students can eat. However, it has only 14 lunch tables. Outside the cafeteria, there are a handful of tables and a few benches with very little shade. The district agreed to provide additional outdoor tables and benches. They cannot guarantee, however, that the tables will be delivered before school starts in September.

The committee agreed to open the outdoor amphitheater, which could easily handle 800 students, as an additional eating area. The committee also approved an allocation of $7,000 to be spent on fencing to secure the campus. The issue of what to do in inclement weather was introduced as a discussion item. It was decided that during inclement weather the auditorium would be opened for students.

Supervision

The group discussed the need to increase supervision during the lunch period. Unfortunately, the district could not afford to provide funds for hiring noon supervisors. The vice principals were charged with assigning supervisory responsibilities to existing staff, including aides, the administrative team, and the counselors. The committee believed that someone should be assigned to monitor the traffic at the front gate. Also, some areas of the campus would need to be closed during lunch, and the parking lot and lower athletic fields would be considered off-limits during lunch period.

The committee suggested that perhaps more than one lunch period should be scheduled. The students on the committee felt that if more than one lunch period were scheduled, some students would attend both lunch periods and not attend class.

Custodial Services

The district agreed to increase the time allotted for custodians to pick up trash and clean the lunch areas. It was suggested that additional trash cans be purchased.

Student Services

The committee estimated that the students needed approximately 10 minutes to eat their lunches and the rest of the time to socialize. As a result, it was recommended that the student body submit to the committee a list of lunch-period activities that would be scheduled to keep the students occupied. A suggestion was made that radios and CD players should be available to students during lunch. However, the committee did not approve this idea because they felt that this would cause more problems than it would solve.

For this case assume that you are the principal of the high school.

Case Analysis Framework

1. Summarize the case.
2. Identify the problem in a single sentence.
3. Select specific information from the case and categorize it according to people, place, or program.
4. Review and prioritize the information.
5. Refer to the data in each category to solve the problem identified in the case and to respond to the case study questions.

Questions to Research and Consider

1. You are hearing rumors that students are planning a walkout at lunchtime to protest the closed-campus policy. What steps would you take in preparing for this event?
2. Do you believe that a closed-campus policy is a positive or negative idea?
3. You have worked hard to develop a positive relationship with local businesses. What impact do you think the closed-campus policy will have on local businesses?
4. How do you plan to address the negative comments regarding the quality of the cafeteria food?
5. If the media arrive at your campus on the first day of the closed-campus policy, how will you respond?
6. Some students are currently using cell phones during class time to order food. Should this be allowed?
7. How would you organize a much-needed lunch intramural program without additional funds?

8. How do you handle an increased need for pest control services because students are eating at various locations on the school grounds?
9. What would be some of the reasons for the board to close campus?
10. Evaluate the minutes from the meetings and analyze the contents related to various categories. Do some categories seem to have more weight than others do?

Developing Your Leadership Expertise: ISLLC Standards 2 & 3

1. Develop a plan for a committee to visit various high school campuses that have a closed-campus lunch policy in place. Assign specific objectives to the committee members for the purpose of collecting meaningful information that would help support your position to close the campus during lunch time.
2. Prepare a press release regarding the implementation of a new closed-campus policy at your school site.

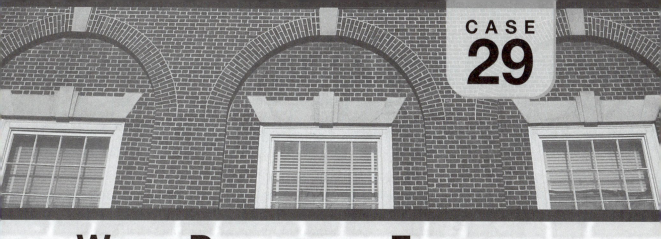

WHEN DIPLOMACY FAILS

The community of Brookside consists of predominately professional white-collar families who live in moderate- to high-priced homes. Warm Creek Valley School District is located in this rapidly growing community, which is situated in the northern part of the state. There are 3 high schools, 5 middle schools, and 20 elementary schools serving approximately 27,000 students and employing 2,500 teachers.

The majority of the parents are college or university educated, and an extraordinarily high number of them participate in school-related activities. The parents are quite conservative politically, and they do not hesitate to vocalize displeasure about programs or teachers of whom they do not approve. Although the parents will profess an uncompromising desire for safe campuses and strong disciplinary measures at all grade levels, many of them will fight to protect the rights of their children to the extent that they invite their attorneys to disciplinary conferences.

The oldest of the three high schools, Swaying Pines High, serves 2,600 students and is staffed by the bulk of the district's veteran teachers. Many of the seasoned instructors distrust the administrative staff, almost all of whom are new to the school. The staff was displeased with the previous administrative team, but they were typically left alone to do their own thing. Some of the veteran teachers believe that the new administrators were sent to the school to clean house and to change the way things are done. Additionally, it was rumored that many of the Asian parents expressed their distrust of the way in which the former administration handled disciplinary matters with the students.

The new administrative team is composed of competent educators. They are optimistic and energized. The principal is very knowledgeable, and his charismatic personality quiets group tension. The assistant principals have various backgrounds and bring diverse educational experiences to the team. All of them have something worthwhile to offer Swaying Pines.

Assume for this case that you are the principal at Swaying Pines High School.

The Problem

Jerry Briscoe was in his first three months as an assistant principal for the school. He had a reputation as a problem solver. As assistant principal, Jerry had developed a reputation with certificated and classified staff as an approachable and affable colleague. Student behavioral problems seemed to be Jerry Briscoe's specialty, and staff members always seemed grateful and satisfied when Jerry handled problems created by students in the classroom. It was the overall feeling of the staff that the campus was safer and more orderly since Jerry's arrival.

Jerry was put in charge of disaster preparation for Swaying Pines High School. Following one of the disaster drills, he convened a meeting and invited community members, a few of the staff, and a representative from law enforcement to discuss the drill.

Mr. Collier, a school counselor, interrupted the meeting. He approached Jerry and informed him that he had just broken up a heated argument between two students. He also reported that he had followed the primary troublemaker to a pay phone. Mr. Collier said that he had instructed the student to follow him to the office, but the student had refused. Mr. Collier reported overhearing the student making a telephone call to request some "backup." Mr. Collier was concerned that the situation would escalate. According to Mr. Collier, the student proceeded to his next class following the phone call.

As Mr. Collier was explaining the incident, Jerry knew instinctively the specific student involved in the altercation. After Mr. Collier described the young man, Jerry's suspicion was confirmed. It was the same student, Dillon, whom Jerry had met in the counseling office a few days earlier. Dillon had been enrolling in school, and Jerry had noticed tattoos on his arm that signified an association with a well-known gang in the area. Jerry remembered thinking that he would have to keep his eye on this student.

When Mr. Collier finished explaining the incident, Jerry decided to invite a police officer who was at the conference to accompany him to Dillon's classroom in case Jerry needed assistance. Jerry requested that the officer wait outside the classroom in order to avoid alarming Dillon, the teacher, or the other students. On entering the classroom, Jerry observed that the teacher, Mrs. Morales, was taking attendance and the students were quietly at work.

Mrs. Morales acknowledged Jerry with a glance and a nod. Jerry explained to the teacher that he needed to speak with Dillon. He approached Dillon and quietly requested that Dillon follow him out of the classroom so that they could discuss the incident. Dillon refused.

The assistant principal was perplexed because students usually responded to him positively when he used this soft, nonadversarial approach. Several more requests were met with the same response. Jerry thought perhaps Dillon was uncomfortable because Jerry was standing so close to him. Thus, he stepped back and again requested that Dillon leave the classroom with him. Finally, it appeared to work. Dillon stood up, took a few steps toward the door and began to follow Jerry out of the classroom.

Suddenly, Dillon reversed his direction, shouted profanities, and insisted that he was not going anywhere with the assistant principal. Dillon lunged at Jerry and, as the other students watched, attempted to punch and kick him. Jerry blocked Dillon's punch and managed to subdue him momentarily. Because of the commotion coming from the classroom, the police officer entered the room and assisted Jerry in restraining Dillon. Dillon continued to struggle. Eventually, Dillon was handcuffed and escorted to the main office.

Case Analysis Framework

1. Summarize the case.
2. Identify the problem in a single sentence.
3. Select specific information from the case and categorize it according to people, place, or program.
4. Review and prioritize the information.
5. Refer to the data in each category to solve the problem identified in the case and to respond to the case study questions.

Questions to Research and Consider

1. Could Jerry Briscoe have handled this incident differently? Should he have anticipated it? Defend his actions or suggest a different approach.
2. Could Mr. Collier have had more of an impact on this situation?
3. Do you have uniformed officers on your campus? If so, how well does the community accept this practice? Would you have asked the officer to wait outside?
4. Would Jerry Briscoe's approach have been different if Dillon were a 120-pound ninth grader or a 200-pound senior?
5. Once the officer gained control of Dillon, what should have been Jerry Briscoe's next step?
6. Which individuals in this case should be interviewed and asked for statements?
7. If Dillon's parents bring him to the principal's office to complain about the bruises on Dillon's arms, what steps should be taken to address their concern?
8. Describe Jerry Briscoe's role in the follow-up investigation.
9. Dillon's mother is from Taiwan. Jerry is Caucasian. Given the apparent lack of trust by the Asian community toward the past administration, should the principal intervene on Jerry's behalf?
10. What legal steps should Jerry take, if any?

Developing Your Leadership Expertise: ISLLC Standards 3 & 5

List the resources available in your area that provide training for school violence intervention. Write a memo to convince the superintendent that you need one of these services for a professional development program that offers training to your staff.

THE CUSTODIAN FROM HELL

The rapidly growing community of Ocean View is located on the northern coast of California. The majority of students attending the local schools reside in planned community housing developments, and their parents pay a special tax to support the parks and schools within their residential areas.

Olympic High School is the newest high school in the community. It opened its doors in September of 1992 with approximately 1,000 ninth and tenth graders. The school population has grown considerably, and the projected enrollment for the upcoming school year is 1,875 students. It is the most technologically advanced school in the district, with a state-of-the-art library and media center, a performing arts facility, and an engineering program.

Although the Hispanic student population is approximately 45% of the student body, the number of Filipino students is growing, and the population of Caucasian students is declining. The student population represents a wide range of socioeconomic levels, but most of the students come from families who would best be described as middle class. Approximately 20% of the students qualify for a free or reduced-cost lunch program, and 7% qualify for Aid to Families with Dependent Children (AFDC). Olympic also receives categorical funding for Gifted and Talented Education (GATE) and English Language Learners (ELL).

Assume for this case that you were hired last year as the assistant principal at Olympic High School.

The Problem

One of your responsibilities as assistant principal is to supervise the custodians. The custodial staff includes one head custodian and six part-time custodians.

Mr. Cush was hired seven years ago as the head custodian at your school. When you first arrived at Olympic High School, Mr. Cush knew that you would be supervising him. He immediately confided in you that his past experience at the high school was problematic because of the lack of support he received from the previous assistant principal.

You were aware that Mr. Cush had not worked well with the previous assistant principal, and you were determined to develop a positive relationship with him.

After a short period of time, however, it became obvious to you that Mr. Cush was not willing to work with you. He reported late to work, neglected his duties, and the part-time custodians became openly critical of his management style. As the school year continued, you met with him on a regular basis to discuss your concerns and, in particular, his lack of personal skills in dealing with his crew.

At each of the meetings with Mr. Cush, you provided him with a written record of your comments concerning his performance. You included in the evaluation of his performance specific suggestions for improvement.

On a Wednesday morning, you arrived at the high school at approximately 6:30 a.m. A classroom teacher approached you with the news that graffiti had been spray painted on the walls of the school. He added that apparently the graffiti was targeted at you. The teacher encouraged you to look at it.

You immediately located Mr. Cush. He was walking away from his office and down the hall toward the parking lot. When you informed him of the graffiti and requested that he remove it before school started, he informed you that he was not officially at work and that he planned to spend the day playing golf. He added that the only reason he showed up at work was to pick up his jacket, which he had left in his office.

You returned to your office and contacted the district office. You discovered that Mr. Cush had not informed the district office that he was planning to miss work and that he had not submitted a request for a substitute.

Case Analysis Framework

1. Summarize the case.
2. Identify the problem in a single sentence.

3. Select specific information from the case and categorize it according to people, place, or program.
4. Review and prioritize the information.
5. Refer to the data in each category to solve the problem identified in the case and to respond to the case study questions.

Questions to Research and Consider

1. What is your immediate response to Mr. Cush?
2. What is your first course of action regarding the removal of the graffiti?
3. Is there a legal issue regarding unsatisfactory performance in the case?
4. What specific legal facts should be addressed in this case?
5. How would you document the sequence of events involving Mr. Cush on this particular day?
6. What policies were violated?
7. Would you consult with the part-time custodians in regard to evaluating his performance?
8. What do you expect the classified union to do in this case?
9. You will be evaluating Mr. Cush at the end of the school year. What impact will this incident have on his overall evaluation?
10. What information should you provide to the district office regarding Mr. Cush?

Developing Your Leadership Expertise: ISLLC Standards 1, 2, & 3

Create a document that would be useful for recording Mr. Cush's behavior. Create a plan to meet with Mr Cush and describe how you would address his behavior. Offer suggestions on what he should do to improve his performance.

The Hip Club Ain't Happening

Τhe upscale community of Lake Olympus has a positive self-image. Although it is relatively new, Lake Olympus is looking forward to the day it can secede from the older, established region to become a city in its own right.

Lake Olympus has three elementary schools and one state-of-the-art high school. Olympus High School has a $46 million price tag and is considered one of the most modern and progressive high schools in the state.

The adults in the community are very supportive of local events; their only concern with the high school is that they believe there are too many students bused to Olympus High from outside the high school enrollment boundary. This situation originated because of low enrollment at the high school when it first opened and because surrounding school districts needed to reduce their overcrowded high schools.

The community is convinced that the problems at Olympus High are caused by students who are bused in from the surrounding communities.

Assume for this case that you are the principal at Olympus High School.

The Problem

Olympus High School prides itself in meeting the needs of all of its students. The school promotes student participation in campus clubs and activities. It claims that more than 95% of the students at Lake Olympus enjoy membership in student clubs. Many of these clubs are sponsored by community organizations.

Sheila Mentor, a junior at Olympus High, is one of the students who is transported to the school from outside the immediate school community. On numerous occasions she has expressed her frustration with the school's policy on how clubs can be formed and who can join them. It was this frustration that influenced Sheila to form the "Hip Dance Club."

In order to form a club, the school required that a teacher volunteer to sponsor the club. Sheila was on good terms with Ms. Johnson, who taught sex education classes at the high school. She liked Sheila and had always appreciated Sheila's enthusiasm and highly spirited personality. She readily agreed to sponsor what she thought was a dance club.

Sheila quickly recruited 10 of her friends and her younger sister to join as club members. She filled out all the required forms and submitted them to the office.

Sheila and the club members held meetings during lunch period in Ms. Johnson's classroom. Unfortunately, Ms. Johnson could not attend many of the meetings. She had complete trust in Sheila and had no problem with the club using her classroom.

Sheila and the club members developed a secret initiation into the Hip Dance Club that required prospective members to engage in a sexual act with members of the school's football team. When Sheila's sister approached one of the football players and suggested that he participate in a sexual act with her so that she could join her sister's club, the football player immediately reported the incident to you.

On the day following the incident, you received a telephone call from one of the major land developers in the area. He was the parent of the football player who was approached by Sheila's sister. The father informed you that he did not want you to make a big deal about the incident and told you to take care of the matter.

You contacted Sheila's parents and informed them that Sheila was suspended from school for creating the initiation requirement for the Hip Dance Club, and you told them that Sheila would be transferred to a nearby school in another district. Sheila's parents informed you that they supported your decision as long as the situation was handled in a manner fair to all the parties involved. However, the next morning Sheila's parents appeared at school with a reporter from the local newspaper. The parents informed you that their daughter was innocent of the charges, and they wanted you to apologize to Sheila and her sister.

Case Analysis Framework

1. Summarize the case.
2. Identify the problem in a single sentence.
3. Select specific information from the case and categorize it according to people, place, or program.
4. Review and prioritize the information.
5. Refer to the data in each category to solve the problem identified in the case and to respond to the case study questions.

Questions to Research and Consider

1. As the principal, what is your first step in addressing the problem?
2. When will you discuss this matter with Ms. Johnson?
3. How will you address the problem of supervision for clubs at your school?
4. How do you deal with Sheila's sister?
5. What do you do when the reporter shows up at your school with Sheila's parents?
6. How do you respond to the football player's father, who contacted you regarding his son's involvement in this incident?
7. At what point do you contact the district office?
8. How do you handle the situation when the community discovers the incident?
9. Do you approach the other members of the Hip Dance Club? What will you tell them?
10. Do you believe that removing Sheila from the school will influence the community's support for school clubs?

Developing Your Leadership Expertise: ISLLC Standards 2 & 4

Prepare a letter of reprimand to Ms. Johnson for her lack of supervision of the Hip Dance Club. Be prepared to identify consequences if she fails to demonstrate improvement in this area.

MEASURING SUCCESS MEETS THE PRESS

Evanwood County is located just outside a major metropolitan city in the northeast. With a population of more than 300,000, the community is rich in diversity and known for its many ethnic lineages.

Most of the schools in the Evanwood Unified School District are balanced in ethnic and socioeconomic terms. The school district has a reputation for its progressive ideas and experimental learning paradigms. As part of a pilot project that was initiated by the superintendent of the school district, two high schools were selected to adopt a curriculum model of their choice in order to compare the models as they related to student performance and academic success. The plan included requiring the site principals to report to the school board on an annual basis regarding the effectiveness of the models that were implemented and how they influenced the academic performance of the students.

As a result, Franklin High School adopted a standards-based curriculum model that closely followed the state guidelines and represented a more traditional approach to teaching and learning. Student performance was measured by tests developed and approved by the state. The principal of Franklin High School, Dr. Lei, was very supportive of this model, and she believed it represented one of the best curriculum models in the state.

Laurel High School's curriculum was developed by a team of teachers, parents, and students under the guidance of the principal. A model was developed to engage students in what the staff referred to as *active learning*. Students were assessed on their mastery of the curriculum by demonstrating their skills through developing student portfolios, planning and completing self-directed research projects, and participating in a community internship program. The students and staff at Laurel High School were excited about teaching and learning.

Assume for this case that you are the principal of Laurel High School.

The Problem

As the current principal of Laurel High School, you have worked closely with a team of teachers, parents, and students to ensure that the curriculum model offers the best opportunity for students to learn and teachers to teach. You are proud of your staff and you have just received notice that your school has been selected to receive an award for being one of the distinguished high schools in the state.

Dr. Lei has been the principal at Franklin High School for the past five years. She is popular with the staff and students. Franklin High School's teachers acknowledge Dr. Lei as an effective instructional leader who introduced the standards-based curriculum model to the staff. She announced at a recent faculty meeting that she was convinced that the first-place ribbons awarded to Franklin High School's students for their participation in the county's academic decathlons over the past three years were a direct result of adhering closely to the standards-based curriculum model.

When an article was published in the local newspaper that featured interviews with five high school principals in the county, you and Dr. Lei were among the principals interviewed. As part of his investigation, the reporter asked for data noting the percentage of students who graduated from high school and attended community colleges and four-year universities or who failed to attend college following graduation.

In the article, the reporter published information stating that Franklin High School graduates were more likely to attend four-year universities than were students graduating from Laurel High School. The reporter published the statement without any reference to specific numbers or percentages reported by any of the principals interviewed.

The article caught the attention of Mr. Pappas, who was on the school board for the Evanwood School District and whose daughter attended Laurel High School. You were quoted in the article and stated, "There are many variables to consider when determining the number of students who enroll in four-year universities following graduation. We do not believe at Laurel High School that all our graduates should necessarily attend college. Our curriculum is designed to bring out the best in each one of our students. Two of our seniors have been accepted at Juilliard School of Arts, six of our seniors are enrolling in the Design School of America, and eight of our seniors have been recruited to attend an architectural apprentice program."

Dr. Lei was quoted in the article as stating, "We have a remarkable teaching staff at Franklin High School. Our teachers are committed to following a strict curriculum designed at a standards-based program that includes specifically designed teaching and learning objectives at each grade level. With a curriculum program model such as ours, more of the students from our high school attend four-year universities than students who graduate from Laurel High School. Standards are important and they allow us to measure the academic success of our students."

The day following the publication of the article, Mr. Pappas contacted you and invited you to lunch. You did not know the purpose of the luncheon, and, although it was not customary for school board members to invite school principals to lunch, you accepted the invitation.

During lunch, Mr. Pappas mentioned that he had read the article featuring the interviews with you and Dr. Lei. Mr. Pappas asked if you knew the exact number of students who graduated from Laurel High School and enrolled in four-year universities following graduation. You responded that you were not certain of the exact number but you were convinced that many of the seniors who graduated from Laurel High School attended college following graduation.

Following lunch, you returned to the high school, and Mr. Pappas arranged to meet with Dr. Halbmaier, the superintendent, in her office. At the meeting, Mr. Pappas reminded the superintendent that his daughter attended Laurel High. He shared with Dr. Halbmaier that he was not pleased with the article that stated that graduates from Franklin High School were more likely to attend four-year universities than graduates from Laurel High School. He insisted that the two principals from the respective high schools report to the school board, at its next meeting, the exact number of high school students who attend four-year universities and community colleges or who do not go on to attend college. He also suggested that the principals be prepared to defend their curriculum models and to prove that they are successfully meeting the needs of students in terms of academic rigor and performance.

Case Analysis Framework

1. Summarize the case.
2. Identify the problem in a single sentence.

3. Select specific information from the case and categorize it according to people, place, or program.
4. Review and prioritize the information.
5. Refer to the data in each category to solve the problem identified in the case and to respond to the case study questions.

Questions to Research and Consider

1. Do you believe that the number of students attending four-year universities following graduation from high school is a meaningful indicator of success? Why or why not?
2. Should the state influence the curriculum taught at schools? Why or why not?
3. Should the nation influence the curriculum taught in schools? Why or why not?
4. What influence, if any, should teachers, students, and parents have on the curriculum taught at schools?
5. Identify what you believe are indicators of an effective high school curriculum.
6. Do you believe that a school administrator should meet with a school board member for lunch?
7. If a school board member contacts you for a lunch or private meeting, are you obligated to inform the superintendent? Why or why not?
8. What influence, if any, do you think Mr. Pappas will have on the superintendent when it comes to deciding the curriculum models that are implemented at the high schools?
9. List the pros and cons of the two curriculum models.
10. Would you contact the reporter and challenge the statement in his article? Why or why not?

Developing Your Leadership Expertise:
ISLLC Standards 2, 5, & 6

Develop a curriculum model designed to combine elements of a standards-based curriculum model and an alternative curriculum model. Present your model to the class and include research to support the development of your model.

BEFORE YOU GO, THERE IS ONE MORE THING YOU NEED TO KNOW

The Rainbow School District is unlike most of the school districts in the area. The employees have remained dedicated to the schools for a very long time, and there is an exceptionally amicable relationship between the administration and teachers. The principal of the only high school in the district, Dickinson High School, has provided leadership based on two principles. The first is to provide quality educational programs for the students, and the second is to continue to offer emotional support to the people who work at the high school.

It is not uncommon to find the district office personnel, school site administrators, and teachers from the Rainbow School District enjoying membership in the same organizations that raise money for charitable causes and donate time to worthy events. Just recently, the Optimist Club worked diligently to produce a play. Many of the district's employees appeared in the theatrical production, which drew a huge crowd and raised $20,000 for the local children's hospital burn ward.

Rainbow is the kind of school district that does not receive a great deal of media attention, maintains a steady reputation for its athletic performance, and boasts of its ethnic diversity. The superintendent and his wife are often seen at community events, and they have recently been nominated as the community's most charitable couple.

Assume for this case that you are the principal of Dickinson High School.

The Problem

Among Rainbow's most noted accomplishments is its commitment to the arts, including the production of plays presented by the high school's drama department. Mrs. Emily Katherine, the department chair, and a dedicated group of parents have produced plays featuring the best of the playwrights.

The community is supportive of Emily's work, and several of her students have pursued careers in acting and starred in Broadway productions. Most recently, one of her graduates was featured in a local production of *Les Misérables*. Additionally, Emily offers coaching and emotional support to the district personnel who participate in the Optimist Club's play, and she virtually walks the actors through each of their respective parts.

Although Emily is known for working long hours and demanding excellence of her students, she has recently allowed her students to leave rehearsal early and arrive later than usual. One of the parent volunteers has noticed that Emily has not been herself lately and that she seems to be tired and not as alert as she used to be. When the parent confronted Emily and asked if she was feeling well, Emily responded by shrugging her shoulders and informing the parent that she was more tired than usual and that she had just recovered from the flu.

About the same time, the superintendent's wife attended a charity luncheon sponsored by the high school's drama department, and she overheard two of the teachers from the high school discussing Emily's health. According to the teachers, Emily recently had been diagnosed with multiple sclerosis and was trying to keep it a secret.

On returning home from the luncheon, the superintendent's wife mentioned the conversation she overheard to her husband. He immediately contacted Emily's husband, who was also a teacher in the district, and asked if what his wife had heard about Emily was true. The husband confirmed the report but did not want the superintendent to mention their discussion to Emily. He reminded the superintendent that Emily had given her best years to the school and to her students because this was what she loved. He believed that she would be devastated if the news about her health was revealed to the students or the parents at the school. Emily had told her husband that she wanted to teach for as long as she could and that she was determined to pursue the life that she loved.

The superintendent directed his administrative assistant to contact you and request that you report to his office after school the same day. When you arrived at the superintendent's office, he informed you of Emily's illness.

He instructed you not to mention this matter to any of the teachers, students, or parents who were associated with the high school. He also mentioned that Emily would have a position in the school district for as long as she wanted to work. He informed you to provide a substitute teacher for Emily whenever she needed one and to be certain to offer her additional support.

After receiving the news, you stood up and began to leave the superintendent's office when the superintendent said, "Before you go, there is one more thing you need to know." He added the following statement, "It isn't often that someone like Emily Katherine comes along. She lights up a classroom and fills her students' minds with wonder." He added, "My son Brian was enrolled in Emily's class four years ago. I believe the gift she gave to my son will remain with him for all of his life. Emily Katherine is meant to teach and teach she will. Anything less would be a denial to other children of the same remarkable experience that she gave to my son. Because of Emily, Brian loves to learn. She helped him find that desire and for that I will always be grateful."

Case Analysis Framework

1. Summarize the case.
2. Identify the problem in a single sentence.
3. Select specific information from the case and categorize it according to people, place, or program.
4. Review and prioritize the information.
5. Refer to the data in each category to solve the problem identified in the case and to respond to the case study questions.

Questions to Research and Consider

1. What steps would you take to provide support for Emily without drawing attention to her illness?
2. Would you give Emily an alternative assignment if she requested it?
3. What role would you take in working with the teachers at the high school to honor her request for privacy regarding her illness?
4. What do you foresee as Emily's greatest challenge?
5. What is your obligation to Emily and to her students?
6. As the principal, how can you offer additional support to Emily?
7. At what point do you speak with Emily's husband?

8. How would you respond if a teacher at the high school mentioned to you that he knew about Emily's illness? A student?
9. What would you do if a parent approached you on the same subject?
10. How would you correspond with the superintendent regarding the special circumstances surrounding Emily's illness?

Developing Your Leadership Expertise: ISLLC Standards 1, 2, 4, & 6

Locate your school district's policy on health-related issues involving confidentiality for staff. Summarize the information and prepare an outline of how you would provide professional development to your staff regarding this issue.

WHEN EAST MEETS WEST

The community of La Esperanza has become a mosaic of neighborhood schools, with a cultural mix of Hispanics and Caucasians. The majority of the Hispanic population has gradually migrated to the west side of the city, and this has caused a separation between the east and the west because most of the "westerners" are Hispanic and most of the "easterners" are Caucasian.

The educational system has eventually been divided as well. Over time, the schools to the west have developed the reputation of having low-performing students, whereas the schools to the east have acquired the reputation of having high-achieving students.

Assume that you are the chair of the Community Forum as you respond to the following questions.

The Problem

The district office and individual school sites have collided in the community because of a state mandate that all the schools improve academically. The school districts in La Esperanza responded to the mandate by replacing school principals in the schools to the west and by promoting growth in the schools to the east. The intent was to recruit new leadership for the lower-performing schools and to build new schools in the eastern part of the city. This news was received favorably by those living in the eastern sections of the city.

The community to the west, however, had developed a strong bond with their schools and their schools' leaders. The people had become unified in their struggle to improve the schools and to bring success to the underachieving student population. Thus, when they heard about the release of so many of their schools' principals, they protested, insisting on justice.

While the decision makers in La Esperanza were busy firing the principals in the western schools and promoting new schools in the east, new residents moved into the eastern section and brought with them an attitude of elitism. As a result, friction increased between the two communities.

As a consequence, a proposal came forward from an interested citizens' group that suggested the establishment of a Community Forum. This would provide an opportunity for representatives from the west as well as from the east to meet and discuss how they could improve La Esperanza's entire school system in response to the state's mandate.

The people from the west believed that they would be given the opportunity to share their concerns and request the return of their school leaders. The women were the most outspoken of the people from the west. They had provided strong matriarchal leadership and believed they knew what was best for their children and for their schools.

The women from the west spoke as one articulated voice at the Community Forum, and they reminded the participants that they were proud of their heritage and wanted what was best for their children. They shared with the audience the high esteem in which they held the school leaders in their community because the school principals honored their culture and worked with the parents to teach the students English in such a way as to achieve success in school. They added that the schools were recruiting parents for night classes so that they could learn to speak English along with their children. The women talked about the dual needs of preserving their native language and, at the same time, preparing their children for an English-speaking world.

The women asserted their desire to improve the relationship between their home life and the lives of their children at school. They felt more parent involvement was needed, and honest discussions between the teachers at the school and the parents of the Spanish-speaking children were critical. One of the women spoke firmly to the group, "Tell us the truth about our children. If they are not doing well in school, tell us. We need to know if they are at the bottom so that we can help our children. It is our right to know." She continued, "Bring back our leaders and let us work together as a close community on behalf of all of our children." The audience listened and embraced the voice of the matriarchs who spoke on behalf of their community and their school leaders.

The women concluded that the school principals had been true advocates for the students and the parents in the west. They spoke at the forum in the hope that the school leaders would be returned to their children's schools.

Case Analysis Framework
1. Summarize the case.
2. Identify the problem in a single sentence.
3. Select specific information from the case and categorize it according to people, place, or program.
4. Review and prioritize the information.
5. Refer to the data in each category to solve the problem identified in the case and to respond to the case study questions.

Questions to Research and Consider

1. How would you describe the problems between the community in the west and that in the east?
2. What would you do to create better communication between the west and the east?
3. What types of leaders do you believe belong in each of the communities?
4. How would you establish the selection process to facilitate a better match between school leaders and parents and staff and students for the schools in the west and the east?
5. Many parents from the east are planning to boycott the future Community Forum meetings. How would you respond to this?
6. Several of the certified staff are planning to transfer to other schools within the district because of the problems between the communities. How can you work with the district on behalf of the teachers?
7. What steps would you recommend for retaining the teachers who are interested in transferring to other schools?
8. Rumors are running rampant in the district regarding the Community Forum. How do you communicate with the community about the issues discussed at the meeting?

9. Many of the existing parent-training programs do not address the issues that were brought up at the meeting. What recommendations would you make to the district office regarding this matter?
10. There has been a steady growth in the population in the east, and many of the newcomers are migrating from the western part of the city. How do you explain this trend? What affect, if any, will it have on the schools to the west?

Developing Your Leadership Expertise: ISLLC Standards 1, 2, 4 & 6

1. Develop a plan that would help to address the polarization of parents in a community and list steps you would take to bring the groups together.
2. Showcase an existing program at your school that brings different groups together and has created a sense of unity among all the members of the program and your school community.

QUICK TO ACCUSE

Smugville is a small community nestled among foothills. The nearest large city is about 50 miles away. The town has a population of approximately 30,000 people. The economic status of Smugville is middle to upper middle class, and the majority of the adults in the community consider themselves professionals.

The community expects a high standard of academic achievement in the local elementary and secondary schools. The students in the schools have maintained high test scores, and high-scoring seniors have been recognized statewide for their achievements.

Student discipline has never been a problem in any of the schools in the district. The school principals pride themselves in providing a safe school environment with very few problems.

Assume for this case that you are the middle school principal.

The Problem

Recently, Smugville was selected by a regional committee appointed by the governor of the state to house two group homes for delinquent youths from the inner city. Each group home would be assigned 5 children ranging in age from 12 to 14 years old. One home would be for 5 boys and the other for 5 girls. The students would attend the only middle school in the town.

After the new children arrived in town, they experienced some difficulty adjusting to their new environment and their new school. The majority of the

Smugville students in the school, however, did not have difficulty deciding about the newcomers. In fact, the students from the group home were pretty much ignored by the student body.

The adults in Smugville have little or no tolerance for diversity, especially when it comes to different ways that children behave. In fact, the community is very proud of its well-behaved youngsters, and it does not tolerate children who do not know how to respect adults and mind their manners.

Your background has involved working with students from the inner city, and you were looking forward to working in a community with few student discipline problems. You wanted to provide a better life for your family in a small town such as Smugville.

When you first became aware that the group homes would be established in your town, you attempted to bring together in a forum representatives from the two group homes and distinguished members of the Smugville community. The response to this initiative was a complete failure. In fact, the only individual who attended the first meeting was the custodian, who decided to stay after work to see what the fuss was all about.

One Saturday morning, just as you were about to head out for your morning run, the phone rang. It was a representative from the local sheriff's department calling to inform you that the school had been vandalized and painted with graffiti. You decided to drop by the school instead of running. When you arrived at the school, you observed that the school office was substantially damaged. Some of the file cabinets had been overturned and most of their contents were thrown throughout the office and sprayed with paint.

A sheriff's deputy located several empty spray cans at the back of the school, which were traced back to the only hardware store in town. When he was questioned by the police, the owner of the store was quick to reveal that he remembered selling the spray paint cans to two young boys from the group home.

The sheriff's deputy and his assistant visited the group home and talked with several of the boys. No one admitted being involved in the act of vandalizing the school.

When you returned to school the next Monday, rumors were flying among the students and teachers. The PTA president contacted your office and directed you to punish the students immediately. Additionally, the superintendent called your secretary and informed her that he wished to meet with you immediately. He demanded that you recommend expulsion for the students involved in the incident.

Case Analysis Framework

1. Summarize the case.
2. Identify the problem in a single sentence.
3. Select specific information from the case and categorize it according to people, place, or program.
4. Review and prioritize the information.
5. Refer to the data in each category to solve the problem identified in the case and to respond to the case study questions.

Questions to Research and Consider

1. What procedures would you follow for investigating the vandalism at your school?
2. What procedures would you set in place to ensure that your investigation does not get out of hand?
3. How would your investigation differ from the deputy's investigation?
4. How will you handle the superintendent's request?
5. Do you feel that a separate curriculum needs to be established for student diversity at the school?
6. Do you believe a meeting should have taken place between representatives of the two group homes because no action was taken at the Community Forum?
7. Do you believe the students from the group home caused the vandalism?
8. What do you believe is appropriate punishment for vandalism?
9. Who would you recruit to help you with your investigation?
10. What steps would you take to rebuild the relationship between the group homes and the school community?

Developing Your Leadership Expertise: ISLLC Standards 3 & 4

Identify the policy in your school district that would apply to school vandalism and procedures for dealing with an incident such as this one. Identify the role and responsibilities of the school site administrators in implementing the school district's policy addressing school vandalism.

TO KEEP OR NOT TO KEEP SAMANTHA?

T he city of Salisbury is composed of an eclectic population. The community is culturally diverse and rich in its multicultural nature. The Salisbury Unified School District is situated in the northern section of the city and currently has an enrollment of more than 25,000 students. Each of the 13 kindergarten through eighth-grade elementary schools is suffering from overcrowding. Students in kindergarten through eighth grade participate in a multitrack, year-round educational setting, whereas high school students follow a traditional school-year calendar.

Olivia Elementary School is one of the 13 elementary schools. It has a current enrollment of 1,050 students, and it is ethnically balanced. Free breakfast and lunch are provided to approximately 55% of the student body. The school itself was built to accommodate approximately 600 students. Therefore, classrooms and playground space are valuable commodities in this overcrowded facility.

Currently, there are three teachers on campus who teach students with special needs. The school is planning to add another special education class for students who qualify. Additionally, there are one speech and language therapist and one psychologist to provide services to all the special education students on all four of the tracks. The administrative personnel include one school principal and one assistant principal.

Staff surveys indicate that they are satisfied with the operation of the school and that the current administration has been very supportive of them.

The certificated and classified personnel are pleased with their contributions, which are improving the educational programs at the school. They do feel, however, that the site has undergone continual interruption because of the ongoing construction needed to update the school and accommodate its increasing enrollment.

Parent surveys indicate that they are also satisfied with the overall school program, but they too are concerned about the continued increase in enrollment.

Assume that you are the principal of Olivia Elementary School.

The Problem

Samantha Toogood is a full-time special education teacher at Olivia. She has been a staff member at the school for two years and has a caseload of 38 students. She has an impressive background working with special education students and is considered one of the best teachers in her field.

Since coming to Olivia, she has had numerous confrontations with the staff. She has complained extensively about one of her coworkers, and she has filed a complaint about the procedures at her site for placing students in special education classes.

Samantha has requested a staff meeting to inform the teachers at her school of the correct process for referring students to special education. She insists that the teachers are ill informed and do not understand the referral process. She also requested to use this opportunity to train the teachers on how to implement certain strategies for modifying instruction for students who need special help in the regular education classrooms.

Another special education teacher, Julie Johnson, is also at Olivia. Julie offered to assist Samantha during her first year at the school so Samantha could familiarize herself with her new assignment. After working with Samantha for six months, Julie requested to be reassigned to a regular education classroom. Julie had been teaching special education for more than 10 years, and she loved her job. She requested the transfer to a regular classroom because she no longer wanted to work with Samantha.

Since Julie's departure from special education, two new special education teachers have joined the staff. Although the working relationships among the four teachers is congenial, the school psychologist and many of the other classroom teachers continue to express concerns regarding Samantha's personal relationship with the staff.

Samantha has continued to work well with the students and parents. She has developed a reputation for having a thorough approach to addressing the needs of the students in special education, and her record keeping is impeccable. Samantha will acquire tenure status if she returns to Olivia the next school year.

Case Analysis Framework

1. Summarize the case.
2. Identify the problem in a single sentence.
3. Select specific information from the case and categorize it according to people, place, or program.
4. Review and prioritize the information.
5. Refer to the data in each category to solve the problem identified in the case and to respond to the case study questions.

Questions to Research and Consider

1. What reasons would you have for retaining Samantha?
2. What reasons would you have for releasing Samantha from her teaching assignment?
3. What would you discuss with the personnel director prior to making a final decision regarding Samantha's assignment?
4. Should you decide to release Samantha, what reasons, if any, will you give her?
5. How will you respond to the parents if they oppose your recommendation to relieve Samantha of her duties?
6. What would you do to work toward a compromise to ensure that the staff accepts Samantha and that Samantha is made to realize that her behavior is perceived negatively by the staff?
7. Does the fact that there are a limited number of teachers qualified to teach special education influence your decision?
8. What can Samantha do to improve her relationship with the staff?
9. List some of the recommendations you would offer to Samantha if you decide to keep her.
10. How does the personality of your staff affect the decisions you might make regarding Samantha's continued employment?

Developing Your Leadership Expertise:
ISLLC Standards 1 & 3

Assume that you decide that Samantha should remain at your school site. Develop a plan that identifies specifically what Samantha should do to improve her relationship with the staff.

THE BUDGET DEBACLE

At Briardale Elementary School, the school site principal, Carl Santos, believes he knows how to run a school, and this includes managing the budget. In the center of town and in the middle of a diverse community, Briardale School also serves as the town's community meeting center.

When a facility is needed for community concerts, town meetings, and the regional spelling bee, which draws hundreds of participants and an audience of more than 1,000, Mr. Santos and employees from the district office support using Briardale.

Briardale Elementary has a population of 600 students, kindergarten through fifth grade. Briardale is one of six elementary schools in the district. The student population for each of the six elementary schools ranges from between 500 to 800 students.

There are two middle schools and one high school in the school district. The high school is well known in the county for its wining football teams.

The majority of the teachers in the school district have been teaching in the school district for most of their teaching careers, and there are few resignations or transfers to other school districts.

The Problem

The school district's curriculum focuses on basic skills and the educational instruction objectives at each elementary school site are based on student performance that supports an emphasis on basic skills instruction. Funds to support curriculum programs are placed by the superintendent in each school site's budget, and the funds must be used to fund the basic skills curriculum.

In the past, the formula for funding supplementary curriculum subjects has led to some confusion and a great deal of competition between schools as to who raises the most money and how the funds are allocated. Foundations have been formed at each school site that are chaired by a parent representative, who serves as the foundation's president.

The funds that are raised by the foundations are handed over to the site principals and placed in a category budgeted for supplementary curriculum programs recommended by the foundation. At Briardale, Mr. Santos has always agreed with the recommendations, but he has—by virtue of an established protocol—forwarded curriculum suggestions made by the foundation to the school site curriculum committee, which is spearheaded by one of the lead teachers at his school.

The parents of the students at Briardale have been very supportive of the supplementary programs funded by the foundation, such as art, music, and foreign language, that are entirely funded by the foundation.

For the current school year, a parent new to the school community was chosen to lead the foundation. When the parent, Mr. Barely, took the position as president of the Briardale Foundation, even though art, music, and foreign language were respectable subjects, as a Harvard graduate, he was motivated to raise the most money that has ever been raised by any foundation in the district so that innovative curriculum programs could be offered in addition to the existing programs.

Mr. Barely was also motivated by the fact that the one of his former fraternity brothers from Harvard, Mr. Morely, was also serving as the president of the foundation at another elementary school in the district; he was the same person elected as class president at Harvard who ran against and defeated Mr. Barely.

As an orientation to the position, Mr. Santos spent time with Mr. Barely and informed him of his job as fund-raiser, his role as president, and his responsibility to meet with the school site curriculum committee and inform them of any ideas that might influence the supplementary curriculum programs.

Because Mr. Barely was used to taking control and enjoyed the challenge of competing with his former classmate, Mr. Morely, he considered himself more than qualified to run the foundation. Hence, he decided to come up with a unique idea to raise money for the Briardale Foundation. He recalled an idea from his former college days, when his fraternity raised more than $100,000 by selling raffle tickets in exchange for a chance to win cash. It was one of the most successful fund-raisers the fraternity had ever held.

After establishing a strategy for selling the raffle tickets, Mr. Barely went to the foundation and proposed his fund-raising idea, and they were all in support of the raffle.

After the tickets were sold and on the night of the raffle drawing that was held at Briardale Elementary School, Mr. Santos and the community gathered for what was supposed to be one of the most successful fund-raisers in the history of Briardale.

What happened next was a surprise to Mr. Barely, Mr. Santos, and members of the community. Apparently, someone from the community had tipped off the local sheriff and informed them that a raffle-for-cash event was being held at Briardale. This tipster knew something that no one else knew.

The sheriff arrived just as the first raffle ticket was to be drawn, and Mr. Barely was asked to accompany the sheriff to the local sheriff's station, where he was booked and released. Later that week, Mr. Barely was convicted of a misdemeanor and placed on probation for his role in the raffle-for-cash event.

Mr. Santos was personally embarrassed, and the raffle-for-cash event and the budget debacle ended up on the front page of the local newspaper and left an indelible mark on the Briardale Foundation.

Assume for this case that you are the principal of Briardale Elementary.

Case Analysis Framework

1. Summarize the case.
2. Identify the problem in a single sentence.
3. Select specific information from the case and categorize it according to people, place, or program.
4. Review and prioritize the information.
5. Refer to the data in each category to solve the problem identified in the case and to respond to the case study questions.

Questions to Research and Consider

1. Do you support the use of foundations to provide funding for school programs? Why or why not?

2. Who do you believe should oversee the foundations and regulate their activity? What are the legal considerations?
3. Should foundations be chaired by parents or school employees? What measures should be taken to ensure that parents comply with the law when conducting fund-raisers?
4. Whose responsibility is it to ensure that foundations or other organizations that raise funds to support local schools are held accountable for the funds they raise?
5. Who should audit the funds raised by foundations and similar organizations that raise funds for schools to make certain that the funds are accounted for and allocated appropriately?
6. What should be the role of the superintendent in overseeing foundations?
7. As the school principal, would you accept responsibility for the debacle?
8. What would you do to prevent this from occurring again?
9. How do you predict the fund-raiser debacle will affect the school's budget and funds available to support the supplementary curriculum programs?
10. What can you do, as principal, to ensure that funds will be available to support the programs that were supposed to be recipients of funds from the raffle-for-cash fund-raiser?

Developing Your Leadership Expertise: ISLLC Standards 5 & 6

Develop guidelines that regulate and monitor foundations that raise funds for local schools. Include policies and practices for audits, and identify who should be responsible for supervising the foundation's activities.

WHEN A STUDENT'S RIGHTS ARE WRONGED

Nottingham High School serves as the central hub of activity in the community of Dover. With only one high school serving 3,200 students, relocatable trailers provide classroom space for the school that was built in the early 1950s. Although major reconstruction projects have brought most of the buildings up to code in terms of state and federal standards required to accommodate individuals with disabilities, due to a lack of funds, approximately one-fourth of the high school buildings remain as they were when they were first built.

Dr. Harvey, the superintendent of Dover Unified School District, has developed a wonderful working relationship with the staff at every school site in the district. Teachers, administrators, and parent volunteers have provided excellent programs and services to the six elementary schools, two middle schools, and one high school in the district.

The community is very supportive of the schools. Over the years, the parents, along with many members of the community, have devoted Friday evenings to cheering Nottingham High School's football team and celebrating its many victories.

Assume for this case that you are the principal of Nottingham High School.

The Problem

A few years ago, Miguel Hernandez and his family moved to Dover. Miguel's parents had read about the success of Nottingham High School's academic program and its football team in the state directory that identifies outstanding high schools. Mr. and Mrs. Hernandez had moved their family to Dover so that their four sons could participate in the football sports program.

Miguel was considered the most talented quarterback at the high school since Joe Amelio played in the 1960s. Miguel was the starting quarterback for Nottingham's varsity football team, and he was the first sophomore to ever be appointed this position in the history of Nottingham High. At every practice, he would show up on time, encourage his teammates to play their best, and remain after practice to talk with the coach about the upcoming games. Miguel was particularly excited about next Friday night's game, as a victory would guarantee the team a place in the semifinals competition for the state championship.

On the evening of the game, the high school football stadium was filled to capacity, and Miguel's parents were sitting in the front row along with Miguel's brothers. Near the end of the fourth quarter, Nottingham was behind 21 to 17. On a third down, Miguel passed the football to a wide receiver, who carried the ball across the goal line for the touchdown. As the ball left Miguel's hand, a defensive lineman tackled him to the ground. As the crowd began to cheer the touchdown and victory for Nottingham High, Miguel lay motionless.

The coaches and medics rushed to the scene and signaled the ambulance. Miguel was transported to the hospital, where doctors determined that he had a spinal injury that left him paralyzed from the waist down.

He was unable to walk and in need of love and support, so Miguel's friends and family helped him through the months that followed as he participated in his rehabilitation program and kept up with his studies.

When Miguel, his parents, and the doctors agreed that he was ready to return to Nottingham High, Mr. and Mrs. Hernandez made an appointment with the high school counselor, Ms. Gusman, to discuss Miguel's return to school. During the conference with Ms. Gusman, Miguel's parents requested that he be allowed to return to school as soon as possible. Ms. Gusman assured Miguel's parents that following permission from Miguel's physician, he would be welcomed back.

At the end of the meeting with Ms. Gusman, Mr. and Mrs. Hernandez informed her that Miguel would be using a wheelchair, and, other than needing access to classrooms, they didn't see a need for any additional accommodations. They added that they knew that Miguel would do just fine in school and that he was eager to return.

Two weeks later, following the medical release from Miguel's physician, Miguel returned to school. Before school began, on the morning of his return, an assembly was held in Miguel's honor to welcome him back. As the high school principal, you presented Miguel with a special trophy to acknowledge his commitment to the football team and the school.

Following the assembly, Miguel reported to his first-period class. His teacher told him that Ms. Gusman had requested a meeting with him and that he should report directly to her office. When Miguel arrived, Ms. Gusman informed him that his schedule had been changed for his third-period class and that he would no longer be enrolled in biology because that classroom did not have wheelchair access. Instead, Miguel would be enrolled in another science class that would satisfy his science requirement for graduation but not necessarily qualify as a college preparatory class.

The following day, Mrs. Hernandez contacted your office to schedule an appointment to meet with you. Your administrative assistant mentioned that Miguel's mother seemed upset and that she insisted on meeting with you immediately. You agreed, and a meeting was scheduled for that same afternoon.

At the meeting, Mrs. Hernandez asked why Miguel had been denied access to his biology class and why she and Mr. Hernandez had not been informed of the change in Miguel's class schedule. She demanded that Miguel immediately be reinstated in the biology class. She also mentioned that Miguel planned on attending college following graduation and that he needed to remain in biology because it was a required course for a university that Miguel wanted to attend.

Before the meeting with Mrs. Hernandez had ended, Mr. Hernandez arrived with a gentleman he introduced as Miguel's attorney. The attorney stated, "My name is Howard Kerri, and I represent Miguel Hernandez. I understand we might have a problem. Are you familiar with Section 504 of the Rehabilitation Act of 1973? Do you understand the implications of denying my client access to a classroom at this school? My client has the right to free and appropriate public education. He needs specific services, and these include access to the biology class and anything else we deem necessary to ensure that Miguel's rights are protected."

Case Analysis Framework

1. Summarize the case.
2. Identify the problem in a single sentence.
3. Select specific information from the case and categorize it according to people, place, or program.
4. Review and prioritize the information.
5. Refer to the data in each category to solve the problem identified in the case and to respond to the case study questions.

Questions to Research and Consider

1. What should have been done prior to Miguel returning to school to ensure that his rights were upheld?
2. How could this situation involving Mr. and Mrs. Hernandez and Miguel's attorney have been avoided?
3. Does Miguel qualify for services under the Individuals with Disabilities Education Act (IDEA)?
4. Does Miguel qualify for services under the Americans with Disabilities Act (ADA)?
5. Does Miguel qualify for services under Section 504 of the Rehabilitation Act of 1973?
6. Are Miguel's parents entitled to a hearing to determine what Miguel is entitled to receive in terms of services and support?
7. Would Nottingham High School, the opposing team's football player, or any other individuals or agencies be responsible for Miguel's injury as it relates to financial compensation for costs related to his injury and rehabilitation?
8. Who would you contact following the meeting with Miguel's parents and his attorney?
9. Would you meet with Ms. Gusman to discuss the situation? Why or why not? If you met with her, what advice would you offer Ms. Gusman?
10. Do you believe that you can come to some agreement with Miguel, his parents, and the attorney regarding a solution to this problem? What are some of the solutions to the problem?

Developing Your Leadership Expertise: ISLLC Standards 2, 4, & 5

Identify the major differences among Section 504 of the Rehabilitation Act of 1973, the Americans with Disabilities Act (ADA), and the Individuals with Disabilities Education Act (IDEA). Include procedural requirements, due process, purpose, who is protected, special education versus regular education services, placements, and funding sources.

A TIME TO REFLECT

Maryville is a quiet bedroom community with a rapidly growing population. Most of the adults in town work in the nearby city of Featherton and commute on a daily basis. The citizens of Maryville enjoy returning home after a long day in the city and spending time with their families and friends in this respectable neighborhood.

The residents of Maryville are proud of their local high school and consider it a safe environment for their children. Maryville High offers its students numerous activities to keep their otherwise idle time occupied. The school has an enrollment of 1,450 students with 1 principal, 1 assistant principal, an activities director, and a staff of teachers who have enjoyed a long tenure at the school.

Although the high school has a population half the size of some of the other high schools in the area, Maryville High has received numerous trophies for football, cross country, and soccer.

Assume for this case that you are the assistant principal of Maryville High.

The Problem

You were born and raised in the city of Featherton. You consider yourself a sophisticated and well-educated individual. After graduating from the University of Featherton with honors and receiving your degree in business administration, you interviewed for various positions but were unable to find a job.

You had always been interested in the possibility of teaching, but you were discouraged from pursuing a career in education by your parents, who felt the salary and benefits were far below what the business world had to offer.

However, as you became discouraged by so many rejections for a job in the city, you reconsidered a career in education. You decided to return to the university and complete the teacher education program.

After hearing about a teaching position at Maryville High, you applied for the position, and on the day following your interview with the high school principal, you were offered a job as an English teacher.

You were looking forward to spending your days sharing with students what you knew about the subject of English and to becoming a part of the quaint community of Maryville.

After you had been teaching at the high school for 3 years, the principal, who had been at the high school for more than 15 years, encouraged you to return to the university and enroll in the educational administration program.

You were surprised that the principal approached you regarding a career in educational administration because you had been teaching only for three years, but you followed his advice and successfully completed the educational administration program.

The month after you completed the program, the assistant principal of Maryville High took another position at a high school in the city, and the principal asked you if you were interested in taking her place. You were eager to please the principal and felt confident that your experience as an administrator would be just as wonderful as your experience as an English teacher had been.

During the first month in your new position, you worked hard and took your job seriously. You considered it a privilege to receive an offer to work as an administrator and quickly adapted to your new role. By this time, you had even convinced your parents that pursuing a career in education was not such a bad idea after all.

Part of your assignment as the assistant principal was to supervise athletic activities. The principal relied on you to supervise all the after-school soccer games because he considered this valuable time for himself in taking care of school matters that he could not attend to during the school day.

One afternoon, just as you were about to leave school to help supervise an after-school soccer game at another high school in the area, Morningside High, the principal of Morningside called your office. During your conversation with him, he informed you that one of the girls on Maryville's soccer team, Candy Vice, had just passed out on the soccer field before the game was scheduled to begin.

You immediately left your office and drove to Morningside High to see what you could do to help Candy and the rest of the team. When you arrived at the soccer field, Candy's coach approached you and informed you that Candy was just fine. He commented that she had probably fainted because she had taken one of her mother's Valium pills just before the soccer game.

He mentioned to you that he had been informed by Candy's father that she often relied on her mother's Valium to calm her down, especially prior to an important game. The father told the coach that he did not think it was a problem for Candy to take the Valium as long as it did not interfere with her performance on the field.

You were uncomfortable with the fact that Candy had taken Valium before the game, and you recommended to the soccer coach that Candy sit out the game. In fact, you suggested that he contact Candy's parents so that they could pick her up from Morningside and take her home.

The coach told you to mind your own business and stay out of his affairs. He stated that in his opinion Candy was just fine and that he intended for her to play the entire game.

You left the soccer field and returned to your high school to report the incident to the principal. When you arrived at Maryville High, you were met by the principal and two school board members. They mentioned to you that they had heard about the incident at the soccer field and that they had already spoken with the principal of Morningside High. They considered the matter closed and told you that if you valued your job as assistant principal, you should follow their advice by simply forgetting the whole matter and not mentioning the incident to anyone.

Case Analysis Framework

1. Summarize the case.
2. Identify the problem in a single sentence.
3. Select specific information from the case and categorize it according to people, place, or program.
4. Review and prioritize the information.
5. Refer to the data in each category to solve the problem identified in the case and to respond to the case study questions.

Questions to Research and Consider

1. What are some of your specific concerns regarding this case?
2. Will you contact the superintendent of the school district and inform him of the incident?
3. What will you do if some of the parents of the girls' soccer team hear about the incident?
4. Why do you think the school board members were at the high school with the principal when you returned to the school?
5. Will you contact the principal at Morningside again? If so, what will you tell him?
6. Will you discipline Candy for possessing Valium at a school function?
7. Do you believe the girls' soccer coach handled the situation correctly? Why or why not?
8. What are the legal implications in this case?
9. What are the moral and ethical implications in this case?
10. Will you follow the advice of the principal and school board members and ignore the incident? Why or why not?

Developing Your Leadership Expertise:
ISLLC Standards 1, 3, & 4

Conduct an inventory of your personal and professional qualities and determine how they would influence your role as an educational administrator.

HERE TODAY AND GONE TOMORROW

Georgetown Unified School District is an urban school district with an enrollment of more than 138,000 students. The district covers a large portion of the city, which includes all socioeconomic levels.

Under the direction of the school district's new superintendent, an Education Academy has been developed to support and promote what the district refers to as "high-performance learning." The focus of the academy is to study teaching and learning and to evaluate instructional practices in order to improve achievement and enhance student performance at all the schools in the district.

The curriculum focus for its first year of operation is literacy, and the district is committed to implementing a specific program designed to improve the reading, writing, and speaking skills of the students.

Assume for this case that you are the principal of Simpson Elementary School.

The Problem

Simpson Elementary is located in the northwest section of Georgetown. The students represent more than 30 countries and speak 34 different languages. With a staff of 34 teachers, 1 special education teacher, 1 principal, 1 vice principal, and additional support personnel, the school functions well.

155

The parents of the students at Simpson insist on a rigorous academic program for their children. Many of them are employed as university professors, professional consultants, research scientists, or technology specialists. They support Simpson's program, which fully integrates students with limited English-speaking skills into the mainstream English-speaking population of the school.

Prior to the new superintendent's arrival, the district received a multimillion dollar grant from the National Science Foundation (NSF). The grant was in its second year of implementation when the superintendent was hired. The funds from the grant were distributed to every school in the district with the intention that the funds would be used exclusively to improve the science and math skills of the students.

The parents of the students at Simpson Elementary were particularly supportive of the NSF grant because so many of them were professionals in the fields of science and math. This is one of the main reasons they were so upset by an article that appeared in the local newspaper over one weekend.

According to the article, the NSF issued a notice to the school district that it was planning to withdraw its grant because the NSF felt that the district no longer had a commitment to developing the science and math curriculum. The article quoted a representative from the NSF as saying that the school district was no longer meeting its obligation to the grant. Furthermore, the NSF had notified the superintendent that it planned to phase out any future funding because of his focus on reading and writing.

You have just arrived at your school on the Monday morning following the release of the newspaper article featuring the NSF story. As soon as you enter the school gates, representatives from the news media, as well as at least 30 angry parents, are there to greet you.

Case Analysis Framework

1. Summarize the case.
2. Identify the problem in a single sentence.
3. Select specific information from the case and categorize it according to people, place, or program.
4. Review and prioritize the information.
5. Refer to the data in each category to solve the problem identified in the case and to respond to the case study questions.

Questions to Research and Consider

1. What additional information do you need, if any, before you speak to the press?
2. Do you feel that NSF made a correct decision? What was the responsibility of the superintendent to inform the schools regarding the phasing out of future funding?
3. Will you contact your superintendent? If so, what information will you share with him?
4. Do you continue to focus on the science and math curriculum in spite of the NSF decision?
5. How do you explain to the students in the science and math program that it will not be funded in the future?
6. What do you do about future staff development sessions that are scheduled and paid for with NSF grant funds?
7. If you plan to continue with the staff development, how will you finance these sessions without the funds from NSF?
8. How do you plan to respond to questions from the parents who are angry about the NSF's decision?
9. What steps should you take in reestablishing a positive relationship with the community?
10. How do you believe the staff, parents, and community will respond to you if you support the superintendent's position?

Developing Your Leadership Expertise:
ISLLC Standards 1, 5, & 6

Prepare a statement for an upcoming meeting with parents. Address the status of the NSF grant and how the withdrawal of grant funds will affect your school's commitment to the science and math curriculum.

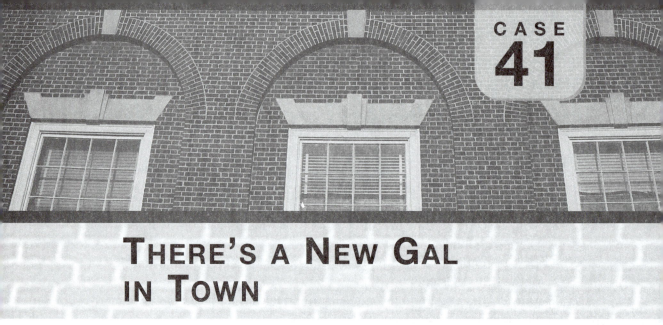

THERE'S A NEW GAL
IN TOWN

The Mariner View School District is a large, urban school district with an enrollment of 125,000 students. Since the late 1970s, the district has been operating under a court-mandated desegregation program that, for the most part, has relied on busing to achieve its objective. Non-Anglo students have been bused to mostly Anglo schools; however, very few Anglo students have been transported to non-Anglo schools in spite of the fact that magnet schools have been created to attract these students.

Recently, the court-ordered mandate for integrating the school district has been lifted, and the district is in the process of devising a strategy to respond to the change. Since 1977, the demographics of the school district have changed from a population of 34% non-Anglo to the current figure of 70%.

When the native language of the students is taken into account, the same pattern occurs. Twelve percent of the student population was identified as Limited English Proficient in 1977. Today 35% of the students are identified as English Language Learners. There has also been a significant increase in the number of children who receive financial assistance from the government over the past 20 years.

One of the elementary schools in the district, Pacific Cove, reflects the same demographic transformation as the general community. The school has an enrollment of 475 students, of whom 68% are non-Anglo. Thirty-seven percent of the students are limited in their English-language skills and represent various spoken languages other than English. At least one-third of the student population is bused to Pacific Cove under the desegregation program.

Assume for this case that you are the principal of Pacific Cove Elementary School.

The Problem

For the most part, the faculty and staff have functioned in a status quo mode for the past 15 years, and they are not motivated to change the way they operate. This includes teaching, interacting with parents, and following recommendations from school administrators. Very few of the teachers have achieved graduate school status; they have been satisfied to be left alone by district office personnel. The school has a reputation for low visibility, a complacent relationship with the community, and student test scores that fall below the mean for the district.

You have just been hired by the school district as the school site principal for Pacific Cove Elementary School. You moved your family to the area recently, and you are looking forward to your new assignment. You are informed by the superintendent that you are the first minority to be hired as an administrator in the school district and that you should feel quite fortunate to have been selected among so many distinguished applicants for the position.

You have been instructed by the superintendent to bring life to a lifeless school, to create a community relations program, and to work diligently to raise student test scores.

You learn early on that the history of the school includes brief tenures for the previous administrators. You replaced a principal who had been at the school for only one year, and the principal before him had been at Pacific Cove for only two years. This apparently had been the pattern for a number of years.

When you first arrived at the school, the teachers greeted you with skepticism, the staff, with suspicion, and the students, with curiosity. After all, they had seen principals come and go, and you were just another new gal in town.

The parents in the community assumed a wait-and-see attitude, and they were particularly interested in whether or not you could relate to the non-Anglo students in the school.

Case Analysis Framework

1. Summarize the case.
2. Identify the problem in a single sentence.

3. Select specific information from the case and categorize it according to people, place, or program.
4. Review and prioritize the information.
5. Refer to the data in each category to solve the problem identified in the case and to respond to the case study questions.

Questions to Research and Consider

1. What is the primary leadership challenge in this case?
2. Describe how you would build trust with the staff.
3. What style of leadership should you use when working with the community?
4. How would you respond to the superintendent who informed you of your hiring status?
5. What would you do to bring the various groups at your school together to form one cohesive team?
6. What steps would you take to improve student achievement?
7. Identify what you believe are the reasons for the brief tenure of the principals at Pacific Cove.
8. How will you work with your school and the community in responding to the recent decision to discontinue the desegregation program?
9. Would you select a teacher-led leadership group to discuss issues with the community? If yes, would you select the teacher to lead the group?
10. How will you bring the various ethnic groups together at Pacific Cove?

Developing Your Leadership Expertise: ISLLC Standards 2 & 6

Develop an agenda for a meeting with representatives from the community, faculty, staff, and parents from Pacific Cove. The purpose of the meeting is to build community support and ethnic harmony.

ONE BILL, ONE BUDGET

The community of Isle Verde is located 10 miles inside the southern border of California. Rich farmland and soft industry focusing on high technology provide steady work for many of Isle Verde's residents. Wealthy landowners and corporate executive officers enjoy the local country club, and the rich blend of Spanish and English speakers creates a culture rich in historical significance and diversity.

There exists a strong loyalty to the seven elementary schools, two middle schools, and one high school in the Tercer Verde School District, which serves 8,300 students. The parent–teacher organizations and annual art auctions help subsidize extracurricular programs. Many of the students in the district have received national recognition for their contributions to the field of art and science.

Assume for this case that you are the principal of Valley High School.

The Problem

Recently, the state passed a bill that was designed to improve the quality of education by reducing class size in kindergarten, first, second, and third grades to reflect a student–teacher ratio of 21 to 1. This ratio of students to teachers was considerably less than what it had been. The bill was to be implemented the next school year, and this left the school district very little time to hire and recruit teachers to meet the new state-regulated formula for the student–teacher ratio. As a result, a teacher shortage had occurred, and efforts were under way to adjust teaching assignments and to develop a plan for recruiting new teachers to the district.

The superintendent appointed you to meet with a committee of teachers, one from each school site, for the purpose of identifying questions and concerns that teachers might express in response to the new bill and how it would influence teaching assignments for the upcoming school year. You established a meeting date and requested that each teacher come prepared for the meeting by bringing a list of their concerns and questions, along with those of their respective colleagues.

At the scheduled meeting, Mr. Borten, from one of the elementary schools, was the first teacher to report. He expressed his opinion that many of the teachers at his school wanted to change their teaching assignment from the fourth-, fifth-, and sixth-grade level to the lower grade levels because they viewed the 21 to 1 ratio as a welcomed change from the 32 to 1 student–teacher ratio that currently existed in their classrooms. He addressed the committee by stating, "Most of the teachers at my school site are close to retirement. The idea that we can spend the remaining years teaching with a classroom of students numbering no more than 21 means that we will have valuable time with them and, quite simply, our job will be easier. This is a teacher's dream, and, if I have anything to do with the final decision regarding the implementation of this new bill, I will make certain that the teachers at my school site who are the closest to retiring have first shot at the kindergarten through third-grade teaching assignments next year."

Ms. Valdez, who represented the teachers from another elementary school, was the next teacher to address the committee. She mentioned that some of the teachers at her school site felt that it was unfair for teachers who would only have 21 students in their classrooms to be awarded the same salary as the teachers who had as many as 32 students in their classrooms. She asked, "Are you going to tell me that there will be teachers in this school district who will have 21 students in their classrooms? This number of students accounts for 21 report cards and 21 parent conferences per quarter. Are you getting the picture?" Ms. Valdez added, "For many of us who teach at the upper grade level, we have double the work; not to mention the middle school and high school teachers who have five times as many students. I don't think the teachers at my school site will stand for the inequity, unless the teachers who have more students in class are compensated for the additional workload."

Ms. Chen, who represented a third elementary school, slowly looked around the room and stated, "Look at what is happening to us. We have been such a cohesive group until now. The only thing we should care about is that whoever teaches our students knows a great deal about child development, early inter-vention, and the purpose for smaller classrooms and improved instruction. Let's not lose sight of why we are here in the first place. It is for the children. It has always been for the children."

Ms. Berstine, who represented the middle school stated, "I am a third-generation teacher. My father was a teacher and my grandmother was a teacher. I think I speak for most of the middle school teachers when I remind this group that the most important thing to consider is whether or not the new teachers understand our culture, what we value, and how we care for one another. How can an outsider understand all we have to offer and all that we have created that has made Isle Verde the wonderful place that it has become?" She continued, "I conducted a survey at the middle school, and there was a common thread that ran through every teacher's response. The teachers at the middle school believe that a plan to increase the number of teachers to satisfy the new student–teacher ratio must include an in-service program to introduce the new teachers to our culture, mores, and customs. We consider Isle Verde a special place and don't want it to change. The current teachers believe that unless the new teachers understand and appreciate the importance of preserving what we have created over the past 50 years, then small class size and student–teacher ratios will make little, if any, difference in the quality of education in our schools."

The last teacher to present a report to the group was the teacher from the high school. Mr. Aiken stated, "It is difficult for the high school teachers to comment on this topic. We have been accustomed to teaching many periods at the high school level, and we are obviously used to having many more stu-dents than you have at the lower grade levels. I was surprised, however, to dis-cover that some of the teachers at the high school have elementary teaching credentials. Although the teachers in the past have always had the opportunity to request grade level changes, now that the class size will be so much lower, I would recommend that the high school teachers be given the same priority as other teachers in the district who wish to teach kindergarten, first, second, and third grades. This is all I would ask."

As Valley High School's principal, please respond to the following questions.

Case Analysis Framework
1. Summarize the case.
2. Identify the problem in a single sentence.
3. Select specific information from the case and categorize it according to people, place, or program.

4. Review and prioritize the information.

5. Refer to the data in each category to solve the problem identified in the case and to respond to the case study questions.

Questions to Research and Consider

1. What questions and concerns from the meeting would you share with the superintendent?

2. How would you prioritize the questions and concerns?

3. What impact, if any, do you believe the new mandate will have on the high school, elementary school, and middle school staff?

4. Do you anticipate that many teachers will wish to transfer to the elementary schools?

5. If you have a teachers' union in your state, how would you expect the union to influence the problem in this case?

6. Should you share what you know about the questions and concerns of the high school teacher with other teachers at your school site?

7. Identify the qualities that you would look for in new teachers hired by the district.

8. Would you invite any of the teachers from the meeting to accompany you when you meet with the superintendent to share the teachers' questions and concerns? Why or why not?

9. Do you personally support the reduction in class size and the new student–teacher ratio for kindergarten, first, second, and third grades? Why or why not?

10. In regard to the district's budget, what safeguards should be in place in case the student–teacher ratio changes in the future and does not reflect smaller student–teacher ratios?

Developing Your Leadership Expertise: ISLLC Standards 4 & 6

Develop a plan for the district to implement the new student–teacher ratio and reduced-class-size initiative. Include in your plan suggestions for recruiting new teachers to the district, research on class-size reduction, and a strategy for transferring teachers from the middle schools and high school to the elementary schools.

WHOSE PROBLEM IS IT ANYWAY?

The community of Willowcreek was originally a rural community with a rich history of farming and cattle ranching. Over time, it has grown into a suburban community with an average annual household income of $35,000.

A study conducted in 1996 indicated that two-thirds of the students lived in single-family dwellings and one-third came from multiple-family apartments and condominiums. Seventeen percent of the district's students receive financial aid in the form of Aid to Families with Dependent Children (AFDC). There are seven elementary schools for kindergarten through fifth-grade students in the district and from 250 to 540 students per school.

Creekside is one of the two middle schools in the district. It has 720 students. It was built in 1923 and was originally the only school that taught kindergarten through 12th grade in the community before it became a middle school. Six portable structures have been added to the existing school. Four years ago, with federal funding, the original building and all the offices were modernized with new floors, carpets, and windows.

The staff consists of 34 classroom teachers, including 3 special day-class teachers and 1 teacher for students who are severely handicapped. In addition, there are 1 vice principal and 1 counselor. The staff is highly educated, and 82% of the teachers possess a master's degree. During the past two years, a technology grant allowed for the construction of a computer lab and the purchase of an additional computer for each classroom.

For the following case, assume that you are the principal at Creekside Middle School.

The Problem

Willowcreek has a reputation for its intolerance of cultural diversity. Recently, a controversial and long-awaited housing project for families of Navy personnel was completed. During the summer, 20 children who were scheduled to attend the middle school moved into the Navy housing and enrolled in Creekside Middle School. Eighteen of the 20 students were African American.

When these students started school in September, they spent most of their time together during lunch and walked with each other during the passing periods between classes. Two of the female students from this group referred to their friends as their "homegirls," and they often wore clothes with similar colors. As a result of their unusual appearance and behavior, the other students on campus began to make fun of them and call them names.

By the end of October, the vice principal and counselor had met with several groups of students on various occasions to discuss plans to dissolve the ongoing tension. During the next two months, numerous fights occurred between students from various ethnic groups, and problems between students began increasing at a rapid rate. In each of the incidents, students were suspended for issuing threats, fighting, harassing, and causing physical injury to their peers.

A particular problem arose when the parents of several of the African American students demanded that the school and the school district protect their children from racially motivated harassment. They had contacted various activists from the community outside of Willowcreek to present their complaints to the district and demand peace.

Case Analysis Framework

1. Summarize the case.
2. Identify the problem in a single sentence.
3. Select specific information from the case and categorize it according to people, place, or program.
4. Review and prioritize the information.
5. Refer to the data in each category to solve the problem identified in the case and to respond to the case study questions.

Questions to Research and Consider

1. What is the first step you can take in bringing peace to your campus?
2. Should you have anticipated this problem?
3. What information should you provide to the superintendent?
4. What consequences are appropriate for continued fighting and/or harassment on your campus?
5. What approach will you take in addressing the parent complaints?
6. If you see that a parent is hostile or becoming hostile, what are some strategies you can implement to defuse the situation?
7. What are the legal and ethical issues involved in this case?
8. Do you think establishing a human relations committee to study the problem would help the situation?
9. What long-range plans are needed at your school to remediate this situation?
10. How would you present your long-range goals to the superintendent and to the school board? What outside agencies might be helpful toward achieving your long-range goals?

Developing Your Leadership Expertise:
ISLLC Standards 3, 4, & 6

> Investigate diversity training used in other districts of comparable size and demographics to your district, and design a staff development plan to include diversity training.

A Slip on Candy, Not Too Dandy

In the community of Stockton Heights, the ethnic majority has changed during the past 10 years from predominantly African American to Hispanic. This has caused friction between the two groups and within the schools. The African American parents feel the Hispanics have taken over their children's school. They refuse to understand why "those Mexicans" want to be taught in Spanish instead of English when they are in America. The African Americans wish the Hispanics would go back to Mexico and leave their school.

Powell Middle School is located in the community of Stockton Heights. Small businesses and single-family homes surround the school. Ninety percent of the students qualify for the free and reduced-cost lunch programs. Of the 1,200 students enrolled at Powell Middle School, approximately 65% are Hispanic, 32% are African American, and the remaining students are a combination of Caucasian and other ethnic groups.

This year, the school was identified by the board of education as one of the 20 lowest-achieving schools in the district. As a consequence, the staff's morale and parent confidence in the school have declined.

Assume for this case that you are the principal at Powell Middle School.

The Problem

A dance was scheduled at Powell Middle School on a Thursday afternoon. The school site administrators were planning to attend a meeting at the district office and, therefore, would not be on the campus. The principal and vice principal were confident leaving the school site because the teachers in charge of the dance had supervised the school dances before and there had never been any problems.

Additionally, the administrators knew that because the dance was held on a minimum day, the school's security officer and other classroom teachers would be on campus while the dance was taking place.

After the dance began, a few of the African American male students invited Hispanic girls to dance with them. A group of Hispanic boys approached the African American students and told them to dance with "their own girls." The boys responded by stating that they would dance with whomever they pleased.

A few minutes later most of the students became bored, and they began throwing candy that had been provided by the Parent–Teacher Association (PTA). The supervising teachers immediately warned the students that the dance would end if they did not behave.

During the incident, a male Hispanic student accidentally slipped on one of the pieces of candy that had landed on the floor. As he fell, he accidentally spilled orange punch on the pants of one of the African American students. A scuffle ensued. One of the supervising teachers diffused the scuffle, ended the dance, and dismissed the students.

Unbeknownst to the supervising teachers, the students had planned to meet on the football field to settle their differences. Within a few minutes, approximately 50 students had formed a large circle around the group of students who had caused the disturbance at the dance. They began to fight.

A school security officer who was nearby contacted the school office to inform them of the incident. He requested that all the male teachers report to the football field to help diffuse the situation. He assumed that the teachers would be outnumbered, so he also telephoned the local police department, who arrived within minutes of the call.

Meanwhile, the school secretary telephoned you at the district office and informed you of the incident. She neglected to tell you that the police had been notified and that the security officer had referred to the incident as a "race riot about to happen."

You later found out that when the police arrived on the scene, the students were subdued and sent home. The police had not asked for any of the students' names, nor did they file an official police report.

The next day, you scheduled a school assembly to speak to the students about what had happened at the dance and to remind them that this type of behavior would not be tolerated at Powell Middle School. You visited every classroom and asked the students to identify the individuals who were involved in the fight. You also asked for the names of the students who assembled at the football field following the dance.

Fifteen students were identified by other students as the students who were involved in the fight. You suspended all of them from school for five days. The 45 students who were identified as spectators were required to write letters to their parents sharing what they had learned from the incident.

The letters were to be signed by the parents and returned to school. You informed the students that if they failed to bring the signed letters back to school they would also be suspended from school.

Case Analysis Framework
1. Summarize the case.
2. Identify the problem in a single sentence.
3. Select specific information from the case and categorize it according to people, place, or program.
4. Review and prioritize the information.
5. Refer to the data in each category to solve the problem identified in the case and to respond to the case study questions.

Questions to Research and Consider
1. Was the supervision at the dance adequate?
2. Do you agree with the security officer's decision to call the police?
3. Given the climate of the school community, what could you have done to ease the tension between students before the dance?
4. For students who did not return their letters signed by parents, how long would you suspend them from school?
5. Should the principal have been contacted prior to canceling the dance?
6. Do you believe the decision to require the student spectators to write letters to their parents was a good one? Why or why not?
7. Do you believe the consequences for the students were appropriate?
8. Under the circumstances, would you plan school dances in the future?

9. How could you have handled this situation differently?

10. What could you do at future dances to avoid this type of incident from occurring again?

Developing Your Leadership Expertise: ISLLC Standards 4 & 5

Research the topic of race relations and develop a plan for working with the students on your campus to address this issue. Include a strategy for recruiting students, parents, and staff to support and implement the plan.

SUGGESTED READINGS

The following suggested reading list refers to the case topics contained in the matrix that are aligned with the ISLLC standards.

Leadership

Ackerman, R. H., Donaldson, G. A. Jr., & Van Der Bogert, R. (1996). *Making sense as a school leader: Persisting questions, creative opportunities.* San Francisco, CA: Jossey-Bass.

Ashbaugh, C., & Kasten, K. L. (1995). *Educational leadership: Case studies for reflective practice (2nd ed).* White Plains, NY: Longman.

Blase, J. R. (1998). *Handbook of instructional leadership: How really good principals promote teaching and learning.* Thousand Oaks, CA: Corwin.

Cohen, F. L. (1987). *From the classroom to the principal's office: Growing pains.* Springfield, IL: Thomas.

Fidler, B., & Atton, T. (2004). *The headship game: The challenges of contemporary school leadership.* London: RoutledgeFalmer.

Hughes, R. L., & Beatty, K. C. (2005). *Becoming a strategic leader: Your role in your organization's enduring success.* San Francisco, CA: Jossey-Bass.

Goldberg, M. F. (2006). *Insiders guide to school leadership: Getting things done without losing your mind.* San Francisco, CA: Josey-Bass.

Gupton, S. L. (2002). *The instructional leadership toolbox: A handbook for improving practice,* Thousand Oaks, CA: Corwin Press.

Mulkeen, T. A., Cambron-McCabe, N. H., & Anderson, B. J. (1994). *Democratic leadership: The changing context of administrative preparation.* Norwood, NJ: Ablex.

Owen, J. C., & Ovando, M. N. (2000). *Superintendent's guide to creating community.* Lanham, MD: Scarecrow Press.

Reeves. D. B. (2006). *The learning leader: How to focus school improvement for better results.* Alexandria, VA: Association for Supervision and Curriculum Development.

Senge, P., & Scharmer, C. (2004). *Presence: An exploration of profound change in people, organizations and society.* Cambridge, MA: The Society for Organizational Learning.

Curriculum and Instruction

Bagnato, S., Neisworth, S. M., & Munson, S. M. (1989). *Linking developmental assessment and early intervention: Curriculum-based prescriptions* (2nd ed.). Rockville, MD: Aspen Systems Corp.

Burke, J. (2004). *School smarts: The four C's of acdemic success.* Portsmouth, NH: Heinemann.

Glatthorn, A. A. (1997). *The principal as curriculum leader: Shaping what is taught or tested.* Thousand Oaks, CA: Corwill.

Henderson, J. G., & Hawthorne, R. D. (1995). *Transformative curriculum leadership.* Englewood, NJ: Merrill.

Kohn, A. (2000). *The case against standardized testing: Raising the scores, ruining the schools.* Portsmouth, NH: Heinemann.

Lewis, A. C., & Barnett, B. (1999). *Figuring it out: standards based reforms in urban middle grades.* New York: Edna McConnell Clark.

Luongo-Orlando, K. (2003). *Authentic assessment: Designing performance-based tasks.* Markham, Ontario: Pembroke.

Tucker, M S., & Codding, J. B. (Eds.). (2002). *The principal challenge: Leading and managing schools in an era of accountability.* San Francisco, CA: Jossey-Bass.

Wilde, S. (2002) *Testing and standards: A brief encyclopedia.* Portsmouth, NH, Heinemann.

Employee Relations

Blase, J., & Blase, J. R. (1994). *Empowering teachers: What successful principals do.* Thousand Oaks, CA: Corwin.

Doherty, R. E. (Ed.). (1967). *Employer-employee relations in the public schools.* Ithaca, NY: Cornell.

Finchum, R. N. (1961). *School plant manager: Administering the custodial program.* Washington, DC: U.S. Department of Health, Education and Welfare, Office of Education.

Hoekstra, M. (Ed.). (2002). *Am I teaching yet? Stories from the teacher-training trenches.* Portsmouth, NH: Heinemann.

Kestner, P. B. (Ed.). (1988). *Education and mediation: Exploring the alternatives.* Washington, DC: American Bar Association.

McDonnell, L. M., Timpane, P., & Roger, M. B. (2000). *Rediscovring the democratic purposes of education.* Lawrence, KS: University Press of Kansas.

Peairs, R. (Ed.). (1974). *Avoiding conflict in faculty personnel practices.* San Francisco, CA: Jossey-Bass.

Race/Ethnic Relations

Abraham, J. (1995). *Divide and school.* Washington DC: Palmer.

Compton-Lilly, C. (2004). *Confronting racism, poverty, and power: Classroom strategies for changing the world.* Portsmouth, NH: Heinemann.

Larson, C. L., & Ovando, C. J. (2001). *The color of bureaucracy: The politics of equity in multicultural school communities.* Belmont, CA.: Wadsworth.

Matzen, S. P. (1965). *The relationship between racial composition and scholastic achievement in elementary school classrooms.* Ann Arbor, MI: University Microfilms.

Myers, K. (Ed.). (1999). *Whatever happened to equal opportunities in schools? Gender equality initiatives in education.* Buckingham: Open University Press.

Noguera, P. A. & Wing, J. Y. (Eds.). (2006). *Unfinished business: closing the racial achievement gap in our schools.* San Francisco, CA. Jossey-Bass.

Purvis, J., & Hales, M. (Eds.). (1983). *The achievement and inequality in education: A reader.* London: Routledge & Kegan Paul.

Romo, H. (1997). *Improving ethnic and racial relations in the schools.* Charleston, WV: ERIC Clearinghouse on Rural and Small Schools.

Gender Issues

Horgan, D. D. (1995). *Achieving gender equity: Strategies for the classroom.* Boston, MA: Allyn and Bacon.

Myers, K. (1999). *Whatever happened to equal opportunities in schools? Gender equality initiatives in education.* Buckingham: Open University Press.

Sandler, B. R. & Shoop R. J. (1997). *Sexual harassment on campus: A guide for administrators, faculty and students.* Boston, MA: Allyn & Bacon.

Sax, L. (2005). *Why gender matters: What parents and teachers need to know about the emerging science of sex differences.* New York: Doubleday.

Student Conduct

Artz, S. (1999). *Sex, power, and the violent school girl.* New York: Teachers College.

Besag, V. E. (1988). *Bullies and victims in schools: A guide to understanding and management.* Philadelphia, PA: Open University.

Bodine, R. (1998). *The handbook of conflict resolution education: A guide to building quality programs in schools.* San Francisco, CA: Jossey-Bass.

Bybee, R. W. (1982). *Violence, values, and justice in the schools.* Boston, MA: Allyn and Bacon.

DiGiulio, R. (2001). *Educate, medicate, or litigate? What teachers, parents, and administrators must do about student behavior.* New York: Corwin Press.

Haynes, R. A., & Henderson, C. L. (2001). *Essential strategies for school security: A practical guide for teachers and school administrators.* Springfield, IL: Charles C. Thomas.

Security, Health, and Welfare

Breckon, D. J., Harvey, J. R., & Lancaster, R. B. (1985). *Community health education: Settings, roles, and skills.* Rockville, MD: Aspen Systems Corp.

Cram, R. H. (2003). *Bullying: A spiritual crisis.* St. Louis: Chalice.

Howard, G. S., & Nathan, P. E. (Eds.). (1994). *The alcohol use and misuse by young adults.* Notre Dame, IN: University of Notre Dame.

Duke, D. L. (2002). *Creating safe schools for all children.* Boston, MA: Allyn & Bacon.

King, E. W. (2006). *Meeting the challenges of teaching in an era of terrorism.* Mason, OH: Thompson Custom.

Kronenfeld, J. J. (2000). *Schools & the health of children: Protecting our future.* Thousand Oaks, CA. Sage.

Rafool, M. (1999). *Funding coordinated school health programs.* Denver, CO: National Conference of State Legislatures.

U.S. Congress House Committee on Education Labor. (1984). *Extending and improving the national School Lunch Act and Child Nutrition Act of 1966.* Washington, DC: U.S. Government Printing Office.

Community Relations

Bennett, L. M. (1977). *Keeping in touch with parents: Teachers' best friend.* Austin, TX: Learning Concepts.

Celebuski, C., Farn, E., & Burns, S. (1998). *Status of education reform in public elementary and secondary schools: Principals' perspectives.* Washington, DC: U.S. Department of Education Research and Improvement.

Larson, C. L., & Ovando, C. J. (2001). *The color of bureaucracy: The politics of equity in multi-cultural school communities.* Belmont, CA: Wadsworth.

Pawlas, G. (1995). *The administrator's guide to school-community relations.* Princeton, NJ: Eye on Education.

Peterson, K. D., & Deal, T. (2002). *The shaping school culture fieldbook.* San Francisco, CA: Jossey-Bass.

Rutherford, W. L. (1983). *In search of understanding their role.* Austin, TX: Research and Development Center for Teacher Education.

Sutherland, D., & Sokal, L. (2003). *Resiliency and capacity building in inner-city learning communities.* Winnipeg, Manitoba: Portage & Main.

Wolfe, L. G. (1982). *Communicating with the community: Keys to school boardsmanship, a program of continuing education for school board members.* Portland, OR: Northwest Regional Educational Laboratory.

Budget and Finance

Alexand, K., & Jordan, K. F. (1973). *Constitutional reform of school finance.* Lexington, MA: Lexington.

Augenblick, J., Gold, S. D., & McGuire, K. (1990). *Education finance in the 1990s.* Denver, CO: Education Commission of the States.

Bliss, S. W. (1978). *Zero-base budgeting: A management tool for school districts.* Chicago, IL: Research Corporation of the Association of School Business Officials.

Brewer, E. W., & Hollingsworth, C. (1988). *Promising practices: How communities across America are working to meet national education goals 2000.* Scottsdale, AZ: Holcomb Hathaway.

David, M. E. (1975). *School rule: A case study of participation in budgeting in America.* Cambridge, MA: Ballinger.

King, R. A., Swanson, A. D., & Sweetland, S. R. (Contributors). (2002) . *School finance: Achieving high standards with equity and efficiency* (3rd ed.). Boston, MA: Allyn & Bacon.

Mosborg, S. (1996). *How money matters to school performance.* Portland, OR: Northwest Regional Educational Laboratory.

Ethics

Cazden, C. B. (2001). *Classroom discourse: The language of teaching and learning.* Portsmouth, NH: Heinemann

Deal, T. E., & Peterson, K. D. (1999). *Shaping school culture: The heart of leadership.* San Francisco, CA: Jossey- Bass.

Kimbrough, R. B. (1985). *Ethics: A course of study for educational leaders.* Arlington, VA: American Association of School Administrators.

McCall, J. R. (1986). *The provident principal.* Chapel Hill, NC: Institute of Government, University of North Carolina.

Strike, K. A., Haller, E. J., & Soltis, J. F. (1998). *The ethics of school administration* (2nd ed.). New York: Teachers College.

Yero, J. L. (2002). *Teaching in mind: How teacher thinking shapes education.* Hamilton, MT: MindFlight.

Governance, Politics, and Law

Adams, N. (1984). *Law and teachers today* (2nd ed.). London: Hutchinson.

Duttweiler, P. C. (1988). *The dysfunctions of bureaucratic structure.* Washington, DC: U.S. Department Office of Educational Research and Improvement, Educational Resources Information Center.

Garan, E. M. (2004). *In defense of our children: When politics, profit, and education collide.* Portsmouth, NH: Heinemann.

Harmer, D. (1994). *School choice: Why you need it—How you get it.* Washington, DC: Cato Institute.

Imber, M., & Van Gell, T. (1993). *Education law.* New York: McGraw-Hill.

McCarthy, M. M., & Cambron-McCabe, N H. (2003). *Legal rights of teachers and students.* Boston, MA: Allyn & Bacon.

November, A. (2001). *Empowering students with technology.* Arlington Heights, IL: Skylight Professional Development.

Permuth, S., & Mawdsley, R. D. (2006). *Research methods for studying legal issues in Education.* Dayton, OH: Education Law Association.

Pipkin, G., & Lent, R. C. (2002) *At the schoolhouse gate: Lessons in intellectual freedom.* Portsmouth, NH: Heinemann.

Special Education

Barnes, D. B., & Barnes C. K. (1990). *Special educator's survival guide: Practical techniques and material for supervision and instruction.* West Nyack, NY: Center for Applied Research in Education.

Burns, E. (2004). *The special eduation consultant teacher: Enabling children with disabilities to be educated with nondisabled children to the maximum extent possible.* Springfield, IL: Charles C. Thomas.

Bootel, J. A. (1995). *CEC special advocacy handbook.* Reston, VA: Council for Exceptional Children.

Chalfant, J. C., & Van Dusen Pysh, M. (1980). *The compliance manual: A guide to the rules and regulations of the Education for All Handicapped Act, Public Law 94-142.*

Coots, J. J., & Stout, K. (2007). *Critical reflections about students with special needs: Stories from the classroom.* Boston, MA: Pearson/Allyn & Bacon.

Jorgensen, C.M. (1998). *Restructuring high schools for all students: Taking inclusion to the next level.* Baltimore, MD: Paul H. Brookes.

Murdick, N. L., Gartin, B. C., & Crabtree, T. L. (2002). *Special education law.* Upper Saddle River, NJ: Prentice Hall.

Diversity

Baéz, T., Fernandez, R. R., & Guskin, J. T. (1986). *Desegregation and Hispanic students.* Rossalyn, VA: National Clearinghouse for Bilingual Education.

Frisby, C. L., & Reynolds, C. R. (Eds.). (2005). *Comprehensive handbook of multicultural school psychology.* Hoboken, NJ: John Wiley & Sons.

Grugeon, E., & Woods, P. *Multicultural perspective in the primary school.* New York: Routledge.

Harris, K. R., Graham, S., & Deshler, D. (Eds.). (1998). *Teaching every child every day: Learning in diverse schools and classrooms.* Cambridge, MA: Brookline Books.

Jacobson, T. (2003). *Confronting our discomfort: Clearing the way for anti-bias in early childhood.* Portsmouth, NH: Heinemann.

Kuharets, O.R. (Ed.). (2001). *Venture into cultures: A resource book of multicultural materials and programs.* Chicago, IL: American Library Association.

Lee, C. D. (1994). *Multicultural education challenges to administrators and school leaders: Urban education program.* Oak Brook, IL: North Central Regional Educational

Laboratory. Washington, DC: U.S. Department of Education, Office of Educational Research and Improvement, Educational Resources Information Center.

McGlashan, P. (1998). *Biodiversity counts: Teacher's guide.* New York: The Museum.

Ngcongo, R. G. P. (1995). *Educational leadership for schools: An African perspective.* Pietermaritzburg, South Africa: Reach Out Publishers.

Sampson, W. (2002). Black student achievement: How much do family and school really matter? Lanham, MD, and London: Scarecrow Press.

Technology and the Web

Anderson, R. S., & Speck, B. W. (2001). *Using technology in K–8 literacy classrooms.* Upper Saddle River, NJ: Prentice Hall.

Bates, T. (1995). *Technology, open learning, and distance education.* New York: Routledge.

Griliches, Z. (1995). *Technology, education, and productivity.* San Francisco, CA: ICS Press.

Ivory, G. (Ed.). (2001). *What works in computing for school administrators.* Lanham, MD: Scarecrow Press.

Kallick, B., & Wilson, J. M. III. (2001). *Information technology for schools: Creating practical knowledge to improve student performance.* San Francisco: Jossey-Bass.

Kent, T. W., & McNergney R. F. (1999). *Will technology really change education?* Thousand Oaks, CA: Corwin.

Scholfield, J. W., & Davidson, A. L. (2002). *Bringing the internet to schools: Lessons from urban district.* San Francisco, CA: Jossey-Bass.

Schofield, J. W., & Davidson, A. L. (2002). *Bringing the internet to schools: Lessons from an urban district.* San Francisco, CA: Jossey-Bass.

Thompson, S. D. (Ed.). (1995). *Principals for our changing schools: The knowledge and skills base.* Fairfax, VA: National Policy Board for Educational Administration.

Conflict Management

Ackerman, R. H., & Maslin-Ostrowski, P. (2002). *The wounded leader: How real leadership emerges in times of crisis.* San Francisco, CA: Jossey-Bass.

Coustiniuk, B., & Shaver (1999). *Crisis management: Keys to preventing and intervention.* Toronto, Ontario: Secondary School Teachers' Federation.

Koch, S. J. (1996). *Conflict resolution in the schools: A manual for educators.* San Francisco, CA: Jossey-Bass.

Lawrence, C. E., & Vachon, M. K. (1995). *How to handle staff misconduct: A step-by-step guide.* Thousand Oaks, CA: Corwin.

Lincoln, M. (2002). *Conflict Management: Patterns promoting peaceful schools.* Lanham, MD: Scarecrow Press.

Ohanian, S. (1999). *One size fits few: The folly of educational standards.* Portsmouth, NH: Heinemann.

Romo, H. (1997). *Dealing sensitively with ethnic conflicts: Mexican American and African American tensions.* Charleston, WV: ERIC Clearinghouse on Rural Education and Small Schools.

Schriro, D. B. (1985). *Safe schools, sound schools: Learning in a non-disruptive environment.* New York: ERIC Clearinghouse on Urban Education.

Thomas, R. M. (2005). *High-stakes testing: Coping with collateral damage.* Mahwah, NJ: Lawrence Erlbaum.

Wolf, E. P. (Ed.). (1976). *Conflicts and tensions in the public schools.* Beverly Hills, CA: Sage.

INDEX